WORCESTER AT WORK

Portrait of a Victorian City

with an introduction by
Michael Grundy

OSBORNE
HERITAGE

© Michael Grundy and Osborne Books Limited, 1997

Published by Osborne Books Limited
Unit 1B Everoak Estate, Bromyard Road, Worcester, WR2 5HN
General Editor Michael Fardon

Printed by the Bath Press, Bath

ISBN 1 872962 71 8

Front cover photograph: The Cross, Worcester
Back cover main photograph: Shop front, Lich Street, Worcester

CONTENTS

Acknowledgements	5
Introduction by Michael Grundy	7
Victorian Worcester – a contemporary account	13
Worcester Trades & Industries:	
The Royal Porcelain Works	21
Lea & Perrins, Sauce Manufacturers	24
Hill, Evans & Co, Vinegar & Wine Manufacturers	26
McKenzie & Holland, Railway Signal Engineers	29
Fownes Bros & Co, Glove Manufacturers	32
Richard Smith & Co, Seed and Nurserymen	35
McNaught & Co, Carriage and Harness Manufacturers	40
James F Willis, Shoe Manufacturer	43
J Sigley, Son & Co, City Steam Confectionery Works	45
Pemberton & Son, Brush Manufacturers	47
French & Boyce, Boot & Shoe Manufacturers	48
Mellor & Co, Sauce Manufacturers	50
Baylis, Lewis & Co, Stationers & Printers	52
R Smith & Co, Brush Manufacturers	54
Nicholson & Son, Organ Builders	56
E J Olds, Wholesale Boot & Shoe Manufacturer	58
Dent, Allcroft & Co, Glove Manufacturers	60
The Bell Hotel	62
The Saracen's Head Hotel	64
Lewis, Clarke & Co, Brewers	66
Joseph Wood & Sons, Builders & Contractors	69
T Bennett & Sons, Photographers	71
Cooper & Company, Goldsmiths & Watchmakers	74
Osborne & Sharpe, Glass, Oil, Lead & Colour Merchants	76
Bowcott & Company, Cycle Dealers	78
J Whitehead & Son, Tailors & Military Outfitters	79
W B Rowe & Son, Nurserymen	81
J & N Nadin & Co, Stanton Collieries	83
The American Dentists' Association	85

Walter Lee, Hatter, Hosier, Glover	86
Bromage & Evans, Builders & Contractors	87
Bulford & Madeley, Provision Merchants	89
G W Y Lewis & Son, Commercial & Fancy Stationers	90
The City & County Laundry	92
J S Cook, Steam Printer, Account Book Maker, Bookbinder	94
Edward Sallis, Cheese, Bacon & Butter Factor	95
Rutter & Jones, Drapery & Mourning Establishment	96
Josiah Stallard & Sons Ltd, Wine Merchants to the Queen	97
W Bennett & Co, General Ironmongers	99
W Stanley Carless, Veterinary Surgeon	100
A M Parmiter, School of Church & Art Embroidery	101
'Gardner's' (Warwick House) Milliners & Fancy Drapers	102
Hardy & Padmore Ltd, Engineers & Ironfounders	103
John Alfred Steward, Dispensing Chemist	105
A O Mainwaring, Family Grocer & Italian Warehouseman	106
C Hancock, Steam Joinery Works & Moulding Mills	108
Chas F Brown, Monumental Sculptor	110
Charles Burden, Botanic Dispensary	111
W Burton, Practical Hunting Saddler	112
W Napper, Fancy Drapery & Trimming Warehouse	113
Bartholomew's Baths & Hydropathic Establishment	114
The Midland Drapery Company, General Drapers	116
Heath & Son, Sanitary Plumbers, Gasfitters, Painters	118
George & Welch, Family & Dispensing Chemists	119
Shipway & Hughes, Worcester Posting Establishment	121
Carmichael & Sons, Coach Builder	123
Munt & Company, Cabinetmakers, Upholsterers, Carpets	124
S Hill, Umbrella Manufacturer	126

ACKNOWLEDGEMENTS

This book reproduces a large part of an illustrated booklet 'Worcester the Faithful City' published a century ago in 1897 to mark the Diamond Jubilee of Queen Victoria. We are very grateful to Elsie Green who kindly gave a copy of the booklet to Michael Grundy. We are doubly grateful to Michael Grundy who has made it available to us and who has written an Introduction linking Worcester in 1897 with the present-day city.

We have tried as much as possible in this new book to capture the spirit of the Jubilee production 'Worcester the Faithful City.' The order in which the businesses are set out follows that of the original. It may not be the most logical order, but its charm lies in the immense variety of businesses described. Readers looking for specific businesses should consult the 'Contents' section printed on the two previous pages. Most of the photographs shown here are reproduced from the originals and many of the design motifs from the booklet are used on our cover and on the text pages. Some of the Victorian illustrations are somewhat murky in quality: we have enhanced them as well as we can.

We have in places supplemented the original photographs and our thanks go to Clive Haynes and to Michael Grundy for supplying these extra illustrations.

Thanks also go to Rosemary Griffiths and Jon Moore for text production and to Anita Sherwood for cover and text design.

Final thanks must go to the original Victorian manufacturers and traders who have made this book possible. Some of the businesses are still operating today in one guise or another; let us wish them well for another prosperous century in the 'Faithful City.'

Michael Fardon
September 1997

VICTORIAN WORCESTER FROM THE RIVERSIDE

INTRODUCTION

From today's impersonal world of giant edge-of-town supermarkets and high streets lined with ubiquitous rows of national chain stores, we look back to Worcester of a century ago when shopping was vastly different.

We have exchanged the intimate scale and intensely personal service offered in local and family shops of yesteryear for what today's expedient and always-in-a-rush society describes euphemistically as 'convenience' shopping. When trolley-pushing with my wife around a superstore, I am always forcibly struck by the growing congestion and impatience in the aisles. Could it be we are starting to see signs of a slowly developing gridlock similar to that which afflicts us on our roads?

Most people seem to accept that this is how shopping must be in our fast-moving world. It is convenient and, above all, money-saving to shop in the superstores and the national chains, although, of course, it all means sacrifice of human scale and is evidence of a great reliance on the motor car.

I can still remember as a boy going into shops such as Beard's Stores in Broad Street and Ferris's in Foregate Street. Distinctive smells permeated these traditional shops, and their window displays and counters were a joy to behold as the years of wartime rationing came to an end. Beard's still had an overhead system of wires which noisily transported those transparent round containers into which shop assistants popped your cash to go to some central accounting point and then back again with your change.

Perhaps, however, such nostalgia puts a gloss on the practicalities. It was clearly not easy for some housewives and older people to hump their bulging shopping bags along streets and on and off trams and buses. Shopkeepers in those days could offer very personal service, politeness and patience but not significant 'discounts' from vast bulk buys nor customer reward or club cards.

Fortunately, Worcester still has a tiny handful of long-established family-run shops such as Pratley's china emporium in The Shambles and Armstrong's, the outfitters in Sansome Walk, but, otherwise, there are few reminders of the nature of shopping that our forebears experienced.

This book seeks to redress that shortfall with a graphic and detailed look back at the remarkable range and variety of shops, trades and industries which graced Worcester a century ago at the time of Queen Victoria's Diamond Jubilee.

All the vintage photographs and descriptions come from a special souvenir book produced by an Edinburgh publishing company 'in commemoration of the Diamond Jubilee of Our Most Gracious Majesty Queen Victoria.' The publication was given the title 'An Illustrated and Descriptive Account of Worcester, The Faithful City.' I am deeply grateful to Mrs Elsie Green who formerly lived for many years at Catherine Road, Worcester but now has her home in Hertford. It was she who kindly gave me this significant book a few months ago.

In 1897, the well-to-do and the country 'set' would have arrived at Worcester's fashionable shops by horse and carriage while everyone else would have come by horse-drawn tram, bicycle (very much the new 'rage'), or on foot. All would have found shop proprietors and their assistants deeply deferential and attentive, desperate to please in what must have been intense local competition for customers.

We can get just a taste of the sort of atmosphere to be found in Worcester shops of a century ago from their advertisements of the time, published in a special supplement from the 'Worcester Daily Times.' It urged 'citizens loyal to the district of which Worcester is the metropolis to support local commercial establishments to mark their variety and excellence.' One jeweller announced: 'My stock, while consisting principally of moderate-priced articles, is yet of good quality and is well-selected and complete. The shop is neat and inviting and reveals the taste and judgement of its proprietor.'

There is perhaps a certain poignancy about the advertisement placed by F.W Weaver who ran the city's oldest boot and shoe shop which was at 84 High Street, a short distance north from the Guildhall and on the same side of the road. Mr Weaver's daughter

Helen became engaged as a young woman to the equally youthful Edward Elgar but she soon broke off the engagement and left for the fresher airs of New Zealand, suffering from tuberculosis. It was an event which had a deeply emotional impact on Elgar for years.

Helen's father's advertisement stressed: 'During its long history, the methods of this establishment have remained the same, and its success has been due to the reliable character of the stock carried. Mr Weaver's patrons include many of the best people throughout the county as well as in the city. The extent to which the business has gained public favour is perhaps the best comment on the manner in which it is conducted.' An advertisement for another shoe shop proprietor declared: 'His commendation of any article is accepted as a guarantee of high quality, and patrons have long since learned to rely implicitly upon his judgement.'

The year 1897 was a decade prior to the arrival in Worcester of Marks & Spencer. The now famous international chain arrived modestly in the Faithful City with the 'Mark's Penny Bazaar,' a bargain-price shop set up in the Georgian property at No. 57 Foregate Street, opposite today's Head Post Office.

A compelling tale of the sons of two High Street shopkeepers is given in the 1930 book, 'Forgotten Worcester' by Sir Hubert Leicester who was five times Mayor of Worcester, a Freeman of the city and a life-long friend of Sir Edward Elgar. Both spent their boyhoods in the 1860s living 'over the shop' near the Cathedral end in High Street, on its east side. The Leicesters had a stationery business at No. 6 while the Elgars ran a successful music shop at No. 10 High Street.

Sir Hubert writes of boyhood pranks by Elgar involving St Helen's Church, across the road from their parents' shops. 'The church's Curfew Bell was rung every night for many years at eight o'clock. The ringer was at one time an old man who suffered from rheumatism.

'Young Elgar, then about 14 years old, acted for the old man if the rheumatism was worse than usual. Part of the duty, after ringing the Curfew, was to toll one of the bells a number of times to correspond with the date of the month. But the 'deputy' took a mischievous delight in occasionally adding an extra number or two to the actual date.

'On many occasions, in order to save the old bellringer from paying a deputy, the young Elgar agreed to ring the bell to call the St Helen's parishioners to the Sunday service. However, as he was due to play the organ at St George's Roman Catholic Church at the same hour as the bell ceased at St Helen's, the resourceful youth started the service at St Helen's three minutes before the correct time, and then rushed off to be in time for his own duties at St George's.'

For a century or more, Worcester held an annual Hop, Sheep and Cheese Fair involving intense activity at the city's Cattle Market and with many shops mounting special lavish window displays, particularly featuring cheeses. Shopfronts were also garlanded with hops.

Through the late Victorian and Edwardian eras, 'The Roaring Twenties,' the Thirties and two World Wars, shops and shopping in Worcester remained on very much a local level with many family-run businesses. True, there were changes in transport with the arrival of Midland Red buses and the proliferation in car ownership and, of course, shopkeepers had to survive the traumas of the Depression and wartime rationing. Advances in science also brought a new array of goods particularly on the electrical front, and the city's population blossomed from 45,000 in 1897 to around 70,000 in the late 1950s.

Otherwise, however, there were no dramatic changes until the redevelopment-crazed Sixties when so much of the established townscape and shopping rows of Worcester were pulled down. The Seventies saw perhaps even greater problems in the wake of all the redevelopment. A desperate commercial recession set in, leaving Worcester with a forest of 'For Sale' or 'To Let' signs on a frighteningly large number of its shops in the city centre and side streets.

Worcester began losing even its own local shoppers as they fell to the lures of much more buoyant shopping centres such as those offered by Cheltenham, Gloucester and Birmingham. Fortunately, however, the Faithful City has enjoyed a remarkable commercial renaissance in the past decade, paradoxically during a time of another national recession which came in the early Nineties.

The Queen and The Crown Estate has waved the most transforming wand with a £85 million investment which has brought the superb Crown Gate Centre. This has increased Worcester's main shopping centre by about a third and brought a welcome array of vital new amenities including 58 shops to cover what had become down-at-heel and vacant tracts in the heart of the city.

Together with smaller-scale developments such as 'Crown Passage' and 'Reindeer Court,' Worcester has largely won back its shopping public of old. A century on from 1897, the city has a reasonably healthy shopping scene though, of course, there can be no recapturing the more human scale and measured pace of times past.

On the trade and industry front, however, Worcester has seen even more tremendous changes. Back a century ago, gloving was still one of the city's major industries with two companies in particular, Fownes and Dent's, each employing labour forces of more than a thousand, plus many hundreds of 'out-workers.'

Other manufacturers of national importance also had their bases in Worcester, including the railway signalling equipment specialists McKenzie & Holland, the producers of suberb cast iron features, Hardy & Padmore, the giant engineering firm of Heenan & Froude which built Blackpool Tower, the world-famous constructors of Royal coaches and early limousines, McNaught & Co., the operators of the world's biggest vinegar and wine brewery, Hill, Evans & Co., the prestigious tinware manufacturers, Williamsons who were the forerunners of Metal Box, the operators of Europe's largest nursery, Richard Smith & Co., the mail order company Kay's, the coal suppliers and now builders merchants, Underwoods, the 'By Royal Appointment' carpet makers, Edward Webb & Sons, the internationally-renowned china and porcelain producers Royal Worcester, the equally famous makers of 'Worcestershire Sauce,' Lea & Perrins, and a string of leading hop factors.

Alas, the majority of these once great companies are no more, except, of course for Royal Worcester, Lea and Perrins, Metal Box, Kay's and Underwoods – all still flourishing constituents of the Faithful City's industrial scene.

From the early years of the twentieth century until the 1960s, Worcester placed far too great a reliance on heavy engineering, with such key companies as Heenan & Froude, Hardy & Padmore, Archdales, H.W Wards, Alley & MacLellan and Meco – now all, alas, consigned to the history books.

These firms had employed vast labour forces in their heydays, and their closure hit hard with considerable unemployment in Worcester during the 1960s and 1970s. Fortunately, however, Worcester fought successfully to achieve recovery and was able to move on from this devastating crossroads. It has since seen a significant diversification of its trades and industries.

Prestigious companies with bases in Worcester today include Mazak, Worcester Heat Systems and Cosworth, though, with the rapid incoming tide of new technology, these factories are far from being so labour-intensive as the large city manufacturers of old.

Overall, Worcester's commercial face is vastly altered from that of even fifty years ago, let alone a century!

Michael Grundy
September 1997

VICTORIAN WORCESTER
A contemporary account

The pages that follow have been taken from the illustrated booklet 'Worcester the Faithful City' published in 1897 to mark the Diamond Jubilee of Queen Victoria.

In a city which blends the past with the present so closely as Worcester, it is not easy to separate the modern from the ancient; in fact, it is impossible, as the former in many instances includes the latter. The old and the new meet one at every turn, and together form a combination of picturesqueness hardly exceeded in interest by any other town in the kingdom. Among the most striking of the public buildings is the Guildhall, in High Street, noticeable for the statues of Charles I and Charles II, one at either side of the entrance, with one of Queen Anne above, the adornment of the front being unique and highly effective. It was built in 1721-23, from designs by a pupil of Sir Christopher Wren, and was restored in 1877, at a cost of nearly £23,000; Sir Gilbert Scott and Mr. Henry Rowe, the city architect, being jointly engaged. The Royal portraits by Sir Joshua Reynolds, with others here preserved, are of exceptional interest.

The Shire Hall, in Foregate Street, is a handsome stone building in the Ionic style, and was erected in 1834-35, the assizes for the city and county being held here. The open space in front is now adorned with a fine statue of the Queen, by Brock.

Adjoining this is perhaps the most conspicuous and handsome of the modern buildings of Worcester – the City's Jubilee Memorial to the Queen, known as the Victoria Institute. This stands on the west side of Foregate Street, and has been recently opened to the public, the institution comprising an admirable Free Library, with Reading and Reference Rooms, Museum,

THE VICTORIA STATUE

THE VICTORIA INSTITUTE

Schools of Art and Science and News Department. The foundation stone was laid by His Royal Highness the Duke of York in 1894, the total cost of the building being about £40,000. Messrs J W Simpson and E J Milner-Allen were the architects.

Among other public buildings are the Market House in High Street, opposite the Guildhall, the Butchers' Market and the Vegetable Market being at the rear – an interesting and much appreciated feature of the first-named is the handsome projecting clock on High Street, with illuminated dials. The Corn Exchange is a commodious brick building in Angel Street; and the Hop Market, a quadrangle of considerable size in Foregate Street, consists of warehouses with offices in the basement, and an hotel.

Other public buildings are the Worcester Government Prison, a somewhat imposing structure in Castle Street, the General Post Office, at the corner of Foregate Street and Pierpoint Street, the Worcester General Infirmary, also in Castle Street - this most praiseworthy institution was built by subscription in 1845, but has been greatly enlarged since, and improved in many important particulars. Other benevolent institutions are the Dispensary and Provident Medical Institution, in Bank Street; the Ophthalmic Hospital in Castle Street; and the Royal Albert Orphan Asylum for the County and City of Worcester, at Henwick. Of charitable institutions, Worcester has good store - some have been mentioned above, but many others are worthy of note. St Oswald's Hospital, in the Tything, was founded A.D. 990, and rebuilt in 1873-74; it is a quadrangular structure in the Domestic Gothic style, the Chapel of St Oswald standing on the south in a large garden; the inmates receive 8s a week, with coals and clothing. Nash's Almshouses, Butts and New Street, date from 1661, the allowance here being 6s weekly; Berkeley's Hospital (founded 1692) is in the Foregate; Wyatt's (1725) is in Friar Street; Shewring's (1682-87) is on the east side of the Tything; and Queen Elizabeth's, Lea's, Laslett's, Inglethorpe's, Goulding's, Jarvis's, Hill's, and several others are to be found in different parts of the city, from which it seems as if Worcester were the very heaven of the ailing and infirm. The Society for Providing Cheap Literature for the Blind, and the St Alban's Home and Orphanage, are also institutions worthy of praise.

In the matter of churches, Worcester is as well provided for as in respect of hospitals and almshouses. Including the Cathedral, the churches of the Anglican body number about twenty, the various other religious bodies having places of worship to the number of twelve or more.

Worcester to-day is certainly not lacking in those institutions which make civic existence in modern times endurable, and sometimes positively agreeable. Amusement in various forms is provided by the Theatre Royal, Angel Street, and at the Public Hall in the Corn Market. The Turkish and Swimming Baths, in Sansome Street, are emphatically one of the institutions of the city which enhance the enjoyment of life.

THE THEATRE ROYAL, ANGEL STREET

Of hotels, the Star, in Foregate Street, an old and somewhat famous establishment, is the most noted. Clubs abound - the Worcestershire Club for gentlemen, and the Ladies' Club, the Union Club, the County and City Constitutional Club, the Liberal Club, and others. Of newspapers, Berrow's Worcester Journal is the leading Conservative organ, the Worcestershire Chronicle, supporting Liberal principles; other journals are the Advertiser, Herald, Echo, Daily Times &c. Music, as befits a cathedral city, receives considerable attention, the chief Musical Societies being the Worcester Festival Choral Society, the Amateur Operatic Society, the Worcester Musical Society, and the Worcester Amateur Instrumental Society. There are also two Glee Clubs, and many other societies connected with Agriculture, Archaeology, Horticulture, games, sports &c. Races are held three times a year, and Regattas are now an agreeable feature of the boating season.

Of course, the great triennial event connected with the city is the Festival of the Three Choirs, which alternately meets at the Cathedrals of Gloucester, Hereford, or Worcester, the last gathering

SIDBURY, FROM WYLDE'S LANE

Portrait of a Victorian City 17

having taken place at Worcester on the 6th, 8th, 9th, 10th and 11th of September, 1896. We have not yet mentioned the many excellent schools of the city and neighbourhood. The Kings School was founded by King Henry VIII, A.D. 1541, and occupies the Refectory of the old Benedictine Monastery, formerly attached to the cathedral, the hall (13th century) being especially fine. The education is classical and general, pupils being fitted for the Universities and the public services. The Worcester Royal Free Grammar School, at the White Ladies, in the Tything, was founded by Queen Elizabeth in 1561; the handsome and admirably arranged structure now occupied having been erected in 1868. A Government School of Art, opened in 1851, is in Pierpoint Street, the late Earl of Dudley having been the patron. Besides these are Bishop Lloyd's Schools, founded in 1713, and Moore's Blue Coat School, founded by a sister of Judge Berkeley and her husband, Thomas Moore, Alderman of the city, A.D. 1626. The Worcester College for the Blind Sons of Gentlemen, founded by the late Rev Robert Hugh Blair in 1866, and formerly occupying the ancient Commandery in Worcester, is now at Powick, about three miles from the city. There are other useful educational institutions, public and private, which space forbids us to mention.

As we have said, the old and the new are inseparably blended in the institutions of the 'Faithful City,' and fragments of greater or lesser antiquity meet one at every turn. New Street and Friar Street contain the chief specimens in the way of ancient domestic and other buildings, among them being the house, already referred to, which was occupied by King Charles at the time of the Battle

OLD HOUSES, NEW STREET

of Worcester, and from which he escaped after the event. Over the door is the following inscription in Old English characters: 'Love God (W. B., 1577, R. D.) Honour the King.' The room in which he is believed to have slept is known as 'King Charles' Room,' and the building, like the other antique specimens hereabout, is in the black and white style of the Tudor and Elizabethan period. The old Pheasant Inn is another example, this party of the city being the favourite resort of the tourist and the artist. But the chief link connecting the present with the past is the ancient Hospital of St. Wulstan, just without what was formerly the Sidbury Gate.

WORCESTER, FROM LONDON ROAD

The 'peaceful development' of modern Worcester has meant an industrial growth not usual in cathedral cities. Some of the chief industries, however, are of ancient standing, notably glove making. Carriage building is one of the modern trades that is carried on upon a large scale, as is also the manufacture of railway signal apparatus. Bricks, hair cloth, tinplate in various forms, boots and shoes of the finer sort, vinegar, fertilising agents, art colours, agricultural implements, maltliquors, flour, with several varieties of the world-renowned condiment known as 'Worcestershire Sauce,' are among the latter-day products of this ancient city. There are also extensive timber yards and steam saw mills within its limits, and the large nurseries of Messrs R. Smith & Co. are at St John's, a western suburb. The hop trade has long been one of the chief factors of its prosperity; but perhaps the most widely known of Worcester industries is the manufacture of porcelain, which has been carried on here for over 150 years. The Royal Porcelain Works, and Graingers's Royal China Works, which together are now carried on by a limited company, are among the show places of the city, perhaps one might say of the country as well, and should not be neglected by the visitor. The show rooms and museum are near the Cathedral, and the processes of manufacture are explained by competent guides, the public being admitted at stated hours on all week-days except Saturday.

'One of the most ancient cities in the kingdom,' Worcester gives its name to the valley in which it is situated, the Severn Valley, being known also as the Vale of Worcester. The position is extremely picturesque, the surrounding country being well-wooded and undulating, and the Malvern Hills rising to the west across the intervening lowlands. The suburbs, especially Barbourne, Battenhall, and St John's, are more than usually agreeable, and the towns and hamlets of the neighbourhood possess considerable interest. Malvern, of course, is famous throughout the kingdom for the charm of its situation, its fine and bracing air, and the many institutions which have earned it the title of the English metropolis of hydropathy. Droitwich, distant about six miles to the northward, is noted for its brine baths, salt works, and commodious hotels. Evesham, famed for its wide streets, antique appearance, and once great abbey, is fifteen miles distant. Ombersley of the many timber-framed houses, is nearer at hand.

Perhaps the most distinctively modern feature of Worcester is the electric light, recently introduced, and now widely used. The long central thoroughfare, which, under many names, traverses the city from north to south, with many of the other streets, is brightly illuminated, and its employment in business premises, private dwellings, and even in churches, tends to become universal.

VICTORIAN WORCESTER, THE CROSS

WORCESTER TRADES AND INDUSTRIES

THE ROYAL PORCELAIN WORKS

Among the chief objects of interest in the 'Faithful City,' and in this respect perhaps ranking next to the Cathedral Church - possibly with some minds even taking precedence of that august fabric - is the extensive porcelain manufactory known throughout the world as the Worcester Royal Porcelain Works. The premises are easy of access, and may be conveniently inspected by visitors to the Cathedral and the Commandery, being almost within a stone's throw of those places of common and noted pilgrimage.

Our limits forbid an exhaustive account of the origin and growth of this great establishment and the important industry here carried on. An adequate treatise, indeed, on the ceramic art, dating as it does from pre-historic times, and abundantly in evidence in Greek, Egyptian, and other ancient remains, would require many volumes; and we must content ourselves with remarking that china ware was first introduced into England in 1631, and its manufacture begun at Worcester about the middle of the last century by the accomplished Dr Wall, who, in 1751, invented the porcelain for which the city has become justly famous. This admirable chemist and judicious patron of art dying in 1776, the works he established were carried on by those who had been associated with him until 1783, when they were sold to Mr. Flight, the London agent of the firm. In 1793 Mr. Barr was admitted partner, the firm's name becoming Flight & Barr. Several other changes in style and title have taken place, without, however, affecting the character or the continuity of the business, the present company, whose correct designation is the

THE 'THROWER' AT WORK

Worcester Royal Porcelain Co., Ltd., coming into existence in 1862. Previous to its formation, an offshoot of the concern, established by a Mr. Chamberlain who had been long connected with the works, was re-absorbed by amalgamation into the original business, a further amalgamation taking place in 1889, the manufactory of Messrs George Grainger & Co., known as the Royal China Works, being then acquired.

The title of 'Royal' dates from 1788, when George III, with Queen Charlotte, visited the works, his warrant for its use having been granted shortly after. Among other Royal visits may be mentioned those of George Frederick, Prince of Wales, the Princess Victoria, Queen Adelaide, Albert Edward, Prince of Wales, the Queen of the French, etc. The works have also been honoured with many Royal appointments, from King George III to Her Majesty the Queen, together with a liberally accorded patronage, a single instance being several splendid services ordered (at a cost of £4,000) in connection with the conferring of the position of Regent upon the Prince of Wales (George IV.) Respecting the Royal warrant, or warrants, for many have been granted by members of the Royal family since the first mentioned (in 1789), it should be said that they confer no pecuniary advantage whatever, and may be regarded as merely a testimony to the excellence of the wares.

A more convenient method of studying both the processes and the product of the potter's art than is enjoyed by the visitor to this Royally favoured manufactory, can hardly be thought of. The large showroom on the ground floor, which is usually entered first, is an almost stately apartment, and well fitted for purposes of exhibition. Here one sees a typical assortment of the company's productions, inn fine porcelain, ivory porcelain, vitreous stoneware (both the latter specialities), parian, majolica, terracotta, etc., an adjoining room containing a somewhat cheaper class of ware. At this point a guide is generally furnished, whose office is to initiate the unlearned into the mysteries of porcelain making, or so much of it as may lawfully be disclosed. The mill in which the components are ground is usually the next objective, the revolving arms and vertical shafts suggesting the old-fashioned grist mill. The grist here, however - china clay and stone, felspar, fire-clay, marl, flint, calcined bones, etc., - differs essentially from the usual ingredients of flour. Next, one would probably be taken to the mixing room, or slip house, where the almost liquid substances from the mill and the clay shed are brought by various processes to the required consistency and homogeneity. In other departments one sees the old-world potter's wheel, and the various operations of turning, flat pressing, casting, firing, etc., by which the articles are brought to the desired shape and quality of substance. To many, perhaps, the most interesting departments are those in which the final touches are added - the decorating room, the printing room, and the burnishing room. Marvellous are the skill, ingenuity, and patience that have worked out the methods by which these artistic and beautiful wares are evolved from their rough material elements.

The museum, on an upper floor, is appropriately reserved for the last stage. Here are preserved admirable specimens of Worcester porcelain arranged chronologically from the inception of the enterprise (1751) to the present date; also a collection of Japanese pottery and porcelain exhibiting certain features of Japanese manufacture.

THE ROYAL WORCESTER PORCELAIN SHOW ROOM

LEA & PERRINS

Sauce Manufacturers, Worcester

No description of Worcester and its many features of interest would be complete that failed to devote a few sentences to a sketch of the rise, progress, and present industrial status of the world-renowned firm of Lea & Perrins, whose celebrated Worcestershire Sauce admittedly stands unrivalled in the market. The business is old established, its history dating back to the beginning of the century. The founders of the firm were Messrs John Wheely Lea & William Perrins, and the present head of the concern, Charles William Dyson Perrins, Esq., the Mayor of Worcester, represents the third generation of business proprietorship. Each of these generations, moreover, have provided a Mayor for the faithful city. Messrs Lea & Perrins' present works are situated in the very heart of the city. Here the manufacturing operations were commenced in 1837, so that in the present year the firm will celebrate its Jubilee synchronously with the Diamond Jubilee of her Majesty the Queen.

LEA & PERRINS NEW WORKS

The works, however, in which the manufacturing of Lea & Perrins' sauces was commenced, have become quite inadequate to the vast demands; and, consequently, with that enterprise which has always characterised the firm's administration, new and imposing premises are now being erected at Shrub Hill. These buildings - of which we present a view - will, it is expected, fully meet the ever-growing requirements of production, and no expense will be spared to equip the establishment with the best and most modern appliances known to the trade.

The output of the firm is simply enormous, and the production of its speciality gives employment to a large number of hands. For the comfort and convenience of the employees, the firm spare no effort, and it may indicate the harmonious relations here subsisting between employer and employed if we say that about one-third of the male hands can point with pride to an unbroken association with the firm extending over twenty years and upwards. Of such a firm words of strained eulogy and commendation would be alike unnecessary and distasteful, and Messrs Lea & Perrins undoubtedly find the highest testimonial to the character of their production in the constantly increasing demand on the part of the public for the condiment with which the name of the house has so long and favourably been identified.

BOTTLING AT LEA & PERRINS

HILL, EVANS, & COMPANY,
Vinegar, and British Wine Manufacturers, Worcester

MR. HILL

The 'Faithful City' presents many attractions to the student of economies, for, besides being architecturally as well as scenically unsurpassed in the Midlands, it is also the centre of industrial activities, which both in magnitude and importance are absolutely without rivals in this country. No better exemplification of this fact could be found than is afforded by a review of the great concern which forms the subject of the present sketch. No apology need therefore be offered for assigning in these pages a premier rank to the firm in question. It has justly been remarked by a literary authority that the magnificent works of Messrs Hill, Evans, & Company rival, both in extent and capacity, some of the great London breweries, and truly it must be admitted that one of the striking features in connection with the enterprise is the colossal scale upon which all the operations are carried on, the various buildings being of enormous dimensions, the plant and other manufacturing facilities being correspondingly immense. As a Vinegar manufactory, the establishment is the largest in the world, no fewer than two million gallons of that commodity being annually sent out by this firm to customers in all parts of the world.

The business dates back to the year 1830, and its progress and development, from its inception to the present day, are among the most striking facts in connection with the history of the firm, nor are there, as far as we are able to judge, any indications that the high water mark of Messrs Hill, Evans, & Company's industrial and commercial success has yet been attained. In former days a public thoroughfare ran through the centre of the works, but was closed some twenty years ago by Act of Parliament, the space being now occupied by a line of railway which connects the works with both the Midland and Great Western systems. The many large buildings have been compared to a great government victualling depot, and the comparison is just. The premises are irregular in construction, a fact attributable to the many additions that have been made as the business developed. The counting-house is a spacious, lofty well-lighted, perfectly ventilated, and exceptionally interesting apartment. A passage of tessellated pavement bisects the room, and on either side is a partition or screen of oak panelling, the style of architecture being semi-ecclesiastical. The carved oak has a substantial appearance, and behind it are rows of desks devoted to the use of clerks. The general office opens into a number of private offices occupied by the principals of the firm and heads of departments.

In order to convey an accurate idea of the nature of Messrs Hill, Evans & Company's manufacturing operations it would be well perhaps to state that vinegar is the result of a combination of the oxygen or sour-making principle of the atmosphere with the spirit that is contained in wine, beer, or other fermented saccharine fluid, and that in entering into such combination one-half of the oxygen combines with the hydrogen (which is an essential constitutent of the spirit itself) and thus forms water,' while the other half unites itself with the alcohol, thereby acetifying it. 'Beer, wine and spirits derive their essential quality from the flavour of the ingredients producing them, rather than from any chemical difference, except that they contain a smaller amount of alcohol, and therefore are less intoxicating than the rest. But vinegar, though intimately related to these, is, as it were, the offspring of them, it being necessary that the fermentation to which the others are due should be pushed to a still further extreme in order to produce this article. Sugar is at once the parent of all of them, and it is from the fermentation of sugar in some form or other that the vinegar is derived. The process, then, involves the extracting of the saccharine matter of the grain employed, and to this end the grain is transferred from the immense granary of the firm, comprising four storeys, and estimated to contain some eighty thousand sacks of barley, the chief ingredient employed by Messrs Hill, Evans & Co. The grain is then thoroughly screened and conveyed by hoppers into the grinding bins, which in turn delivers the malt to six pairs of large French millstones which pulverize it effectually. The meal is then transferred to a wooden trough, when by rotating pockets attached to a leather band it is conveyed to a floor above the gigantic mash tun, a cask capable of holding 12,307 gallons. In this vessel aromatic, glutinous 'sweet wort' is produced and in turn this is converted into 'gyle.' Messrs Hill, Evans & Company's fermenting room contains eleven vats, each with a 15,000 gallons capacity, while another mammoth vat in the same room will hold 30,000 gallons. But to realise what can be done in the art of gigantic cask making one must visit the storage room in which will be found a cask capable of holding 114,821 gallons. This is undoubtedly the largest vat in the world. The cooperage also is worthy of a visit, and here a very large staff is employed in addition to mechanical appliances of the most improved type. Fire engine department and filling rooms are also deeply interesting, but space prevents our giving a detailed account of them.

Turning our attention to the firm's British wine manufacture we may remark that Messrs Hill, Evans & Co. have always been celebrated for the superior quality of these beverages produced by them. The firm use only fruits of the highest quality, and in the manufacture no adulteration by means of deleterous compounds is permitted. The firm make an excellent British port and sherry, not to mention orange, gooseberry, raising, ginger, currant, cowslip, cherry, etc. The house is one of which the 'Faithful City' may well be proud, and it contributes enormously to the social well being of the community amid which its operations are conducted.

MESSRS. McKENZIE & HOLLAND
Railway Signal Engineers,
Vulcan Iron Works, Worcester

When we consider the thousands of trains which daily rush, at enormous speeds, hither and thither, over our intricate railway system, it is truly wonderful that the death roll from accidents should be as insignificant as it is at present. Indeed it is computed, by those best able to form an opinion, that the risk of danger to life or limb is less to the traveller in an express train, running sixty miles an hour, than to the ordinary pedestrian leisurely walking through the streets of our great cities. This satisfactory state of affairs is of course due to the perfection of the signalling operations adopted on our best lines - arrangements which it has taken more than half-a-century of thought and ingenuity to bring to their present position. The ancient city of Worcester is associated in the minds of the majority of people with the manufacture of gloves, sauce, porcelain, and it may comes as a surprise to the general

MCKENZIE & HOLLAND RAILWAY SIGNALS

public to learn that they owe no small measure of their immunity from railway accidents to a firm located in this pleasant city, on the banks of the Severn. Railway men, however, all the world over, know well, and fully appreciate the remarkable services of Messrs McKenzie & Holland of Worcester in Railway Signalling work, for wherever a complicated system of rails exist, be it in England, in Australia, India, Egypt or the Argentine, their engineers have had reason to bless the inventors of the 'Interlocking' system. Amongst the first and foremost, are none other than the firm under notice, for we take the true inventors to be those who first put an idea into practical working order. Space precludes our entering into any detailed account of this ingenious system, beyond remarking that

MCKENZIE & HOLLAND SIGNAL GANTRY

by means of it, the signalman is relieved from nine-tenths of his responsibilities, and is prevented from making mistakes by reason of the immutability of the levers which he operates. The mere act of lowering a signal for a train to pass locks and makes immovable all the points over which the train must pass, as well as any points or signals which may conflict with the incoming road. The locking is automatic, and it is the business of the engineer to devise the details of the apparatus, which secures that this result shall follow the pulling of the lever in the box. If, on the other hand, a train is going out of one of the bays, it is impossible for the signalman to lower the signal which permits the train to start until the points over which the train has to travel are set in the proper position. The almost perfectness of this admirable system has been developed by the firm of Messrs McKenzie & Holland of Worcester, who have provided some of the largest installations of the kind in the world. Among these we may mention Newcastle Station on the North Eastern Railway, which contains no fewer than 524 interlocking levers. In No. 1 Cabin there is certainly one of the largest locking frames in one length in existence, as it contains 244 levers, and is 80 or 90 feet long. At Liverpool Street, London, terminus of the Great Eastern Railway, there are two large signal cabins, the West Box containing 240 levers, and the East Box 136 levers, and it is calculated that no less than 1100 trains pass in and out of the station daily. This firm also undertakes contracts on the Telegraph Block System, they being the sole licensees of Sykes Electric Block Locking, the most perfect device of the kind known to engineers, and of the Westinghouse Electric Pneumatic System of Signalling, which has been so successfully in use in the United States of America for some years.

Messrs McKenzie & Holland's works constitute the largest industrial institution in Worcester, and they are also the most extensive employers of labour, having about 600 work people. The Vulcan Iron Works cover an area of about 4 acres, and are situated on both sides of the Birmingham and Worcester Canal. They also have a siding from the Great Western Railway, which affords capital facilities for transport purposes. The works are admirably organised and equipped with the most modern machinery and labour saving appliances. There is a fine foundry, also a saw mill fitted with the most improved wood working machinery, engineer's shops with powerful machine tools, etc. They have also corresponding works in Australia, notably at Melbourne and Brisbane.

The firm was founded in 1862, and the present proprietor is Walter Holland, Esq., of Rose Hill, Worcester. He is a prominent figure in social and commercial circles in Worcestershire. He was Mayor of the City 1891-92, and has been an Alderman for some years, and is a Justice of the Peace for the City and County and a Deputy-Lieutenant of the County.

MESSRS. FOWNES BROS. & CO.,
Glove Manufacturers

For upwards of a century past no name has been more familiarly identified with Worcester's chief staple industry than that of Messrs. Fownes Bros. & Co., whose manufacture of gloves is to-day of world-wide significance and repute. The origin of the business dates back to its foundation in Worcester in 1777 by Mr. John Fownes, who subsequently removed to Hanwell, and in succeeding years established a large factory in the suburbs of London to meet the always increasing demand for the gloves of the firm's make.

In 1884, the then proprietors determined to concentrate their manufactures in the parent home of the industry, and at that date inaugurated the present handsome and commodious buildings, erected on the commanding site at the corner of Talbot and Clare

FOWNES GLOVES MANUFACTURY

Streets, in the part of the city known as the 'Blockhouse' on the Worcester and Birmingham canal. The extensive past experience of the firm is evidenced in the efficiency of the design and arrangement of the factory; the lighting, ventilation, and sanitation being alike perfect in every detail calculated to add to the health and comfort of the employees. The mechanical equipment throughout is of the best, and includes all the most up-to-date improvements in steam power machines for sewing; and the engineers' department, where all the necessary repairs are carried out. It would be outside the province of this work to describe in detail the various stages of preparation and manufacture, from the raw material to the finished glove, and we therefore direct attention to an inspection of the stock rooms, where are on view samples of the immense number of various kinds of goods produced by the firm. These include gloves of every description for children's, ladies', and men's wear, from the humble thread glove to the finest quality of Paris-made glace kid and Suede. There is an endless variety of colourings, including the very latest dress shades, finished in various styles of buttons and embroideries to suit all tastes and markets. Lined gloves are without doubt an important speciality of this firm, and are made in real fur, reindeer, lamb, Cape and Chevrette, with rich linings of fur, pure cashmere, etc., which betoken warmth and comfort, combined with durability. Woollen gloves are also largely represented, machine knitting having been brought to such perfection that it has almost entirely superseded hand labour.

The Worcester factory is, however, essentially the industrial headquarters of the leather glove trade of the firm, but at their London warehouse, another important department is devoted exclusively to makes of leather gloves, entirely distinct in character from those made at Worcester, comprising walking and driving gloves and the 'buckskins' for military purposes. This department produces the well-known makes of 'Nantwich Gauntlets,' a popular wear for ladies and children in the country, lawn tennis, cycling, and other out-door recreations. The fabric gloves of silk, thread, cashmere, and other materials, except leather, are manufactured at Messrs. Fownes' factories at Taunton and Torrington, solely confined to this branch of the industry.

An interesting feature of the business, especially worthy of note, in view of the approaching Diamond Jubilee of her Majesty's long and prosperous reign, is the fact that visitors are shown the pattern sizes of gloves always kept in stock for the Queen and members of the Royal Family. The London warehouses of the firm are at 71, 73 and 75, Gresham Street, and 1, Aldermanbury, and a branch establishment has been recently opened at 39 to 41, East 12th Street, New York, under the supervision of Mr. Ernest Smellie, from the city headquarters. The firm has an agency with Messrs. Gault Bros. of Montreal; while the Australian trade is well-developed by Messrs. Cox and Mailer, Salisbury Buildings, Bourke Street, West, Melbourne Victoria; and they have also representatives in all the principal centres on the Continent, the Colonies, and South America.

Many hundreds of hands are employed in the vast industry controlled by Messrs. Fownes, who evidence the close personal interest they take in the welfare of their work people by providing for their hours of recreation a comfortable and well-equipped club-house, erected on a site opposite the factory, and, needless to add, substantially appreciated by those for whose pleasure it was designed.

FOWNES GLOVES – PREPARING THE LEATHER

RICHARD SMITH & CO.
Seed and Nurserymen, St. John's Nursery, and Broad Street and High Street, Worcester.

The importance of Worcester as a centre of the seed and nursery industries of England is nowhere more strikingly or more conclusively attested than at the great establishment which forms the subject of the present sketch; indeed, no record of Worcester's historical, descriptive, and industrial development during the past half century would be complete that omitted a comprehensive account of Messrs. Richard Smith & Company's famous nurseries.

This business, which, in respect of magnitude, probably stands unrivalled in the Western Midlands, was originally founded by the late Mr. Richard Smith, in the year 1804. Organised on extremely modest lines at the outset, the founder by indomitable perseverance and industry, allied to a character of unimpreachable integrity, built up during his own lifetime a splendid business; nor have the same high commercial aims and ideals been absent characteristics in those who subsequently assumed the direction of the enterprise.

The nurseries are situate at St. John's, on the opposite side of the Severn than is the Cathedral, and are reached by tram. The great broad drive is a mile in length, the cross drives are seven-eighths of a mile, and the entire nursery includes no fewer than thirty-three miles of pathway. The building, now used as the general office, was formerly the residence of the founder - it is a pretty place, albeit no longer employed for more attractive purposes than clerical work connected with an exceptionally artistic and scientific calling, and its creeper-clad walls and environment of ornamental shrubs can hardly fail to impress the visitor. After calling upon the gentleman in charge here, the natural question arises in one's mind, 'where to begin' a tour of inspection of the vast area, with its almost infinite floricultural and kindred resources. Let us begin with the roses, which occupy some twelve acres thickly planted with healthly trees. Messrs. Richard Smith & Co. have cultivated roses with the greatest success for the past ninety years, have sent them to almost every part of the world, and have given universal satisfaction to patrons. In the long

RICHARD SMITH & CO – THE GLASSHOUSES

catalogue of the firm's roses, all the sorts are of acknowledged excellence, inferior classes being systematically and immediately discarded on the imperfection being recognised. The rose quarter at St. John's is a veritable revelation of choice things, and we can only regret that space does not admit of our mentioning in detail some of the specialties that attracted our attention.

Turning next our notice to the growth of fruit trees, we find that the firm devote no fewer than eighty acres to this department of operations. Among apples we may specialize:- Early Desert, Worcester Pearman, White Transparent, Lady Margaret, Irish Peach, Early Kitchen, Lord Suffield, Ecklinville Seedling, Cellini, Stirling Castle, and many other varieties are no less deserving of commendation. The list of pears is no less comprehensive and worthy of praise, while peaches, nectarines, apricots, plums, gooseberries, raspberries, and currant trees of every hue and character are numerically represented in a manner that would make many a great European standing army look insignificant so far as numbers are concerned. And what shall we say about the acres of beech, silverleaved poplar, scarlet American oaks, Virginian creepers, thorns, fern-leaved weeping birches, fern-leaved limes, ash, willows, and other trees.

The houses next claim attention. Here order, cleanliness, and perfect organisation prevail in a pre-eminent degree. There are more than twenty houses, and one of them measures 365 feet in length. The pit ground covers four acres, two and three quarter acres being under glass. In the fern house may be found 20,000 plants in pots; in the vineries, 4000 vines; while heaths camellias, chrysanthemums, and a thousand other varieties of flower and leaf are simply beyond our power of description.

The seed trade of the firm yet remains to be referred to, and here we may say that one of Messrs. Smith & Co.'s greatest sources of success achieved, and of the foundation of confidence inspired among their customers is attributable to the firm's desire only to sell goods as represented, grown from well-recognised stocks, and to the extreme care taken in their selection. Few persons, and only those intimately acquainted with this important branch, are aware of the trouble, time, and expense involved in procuring stocks of a high quality, Messrs. Richard Smith & Co. possess exceptional opportunities for acquiring the choicest stocks of the leading vegetable and farm seeds - and the utmost personal attention is

RICHARD SMITH & CO – THE ST JOHNS NURSERY

given to this branch. Having secured the best types of the respective seeds, these are carefully tested under proper conditions in order to ensure that the germination power is good. These are again sown and cultivated in the firm's trial grounds to prove the precise character of the different stocks, and the results in each case are carefully registered for reference.

Among Messrs. Smith & Co.'s vegetable seeds are numbered choice varieties of garden peas, beans, cabbages, carrots, turnips, beets, brussel sprouts, savoys, celeries, and seedling potatoes. Honours in-numerable have been won at all the leading Exhibitions of the country. In farm root seeds, Messrs. Smith stand extremely high, many of the varieties of roots having achieved world-wide celebrity.

Amongst turnips are several varieties of a quality unsurpassed. The clover and grass seeds department has grown to large proportions, and for many years the firm has devoted close attention to the proper selection of grasses, clover, etc., for alternate husbandry, and more particularly to those varied natural grasses best suited for laying down land to permanent pasture or meadow,

THE ST JOHNS NURSERY – SPECIMEN TREES

Portrait of a Victorian City

RICHARD SMITH & CO – FIELD LABOURERS

ornamental parks, cricket, football, and tennis grounds. The unsolicited testimony of leading customers eloquently indicate the success achieved. In concluding this notice of a popular Worcester enterprise, it may be mentioned that the scope of operation is world-wide, the clientele numerically enormous, including as it does, names such as one would naturally imagine exhausted the list of titled personages given in the publications of a Debrett or a Burke. It is such firms as the one under notice that maintain the prestige of British commerce, and that contribute in more than a merely literal sense to effect that happy consummation of which Dean Swift spoke when he said, that 'he who makes two blades of grass to grow where one grew before is a philanthropist, and of more service to his kind than all the bands of philosophers and politicians put together.'

McNAUGHT & CO.
Carriage and Harness Manufacturers, Worcester

A well-known *litterateur* has justly emphasised the fact that England is *par excellence* the centre of the coach building industry, and certainly the perfection to which the art has been brought in this country attracts the admiration of competent critics in every part of the civilised world. Foremost among the great coach building enterprises that have contributed to this proud National distinction, we do not hesitate to rank the firm we name at the head of this necessarily brief sketch. It is more than a century since the firm was founded, and, from the date of its inception to the present hour, 'progress' has been the watchword that has continuously animated the administration of the firms affairs. In 1862 Messrs. McNaught first essayed public competition, and then, as at all subsequent Exhibitions, the firm has secured the highest awards. Among these trophies testifying to the quality of material, workmanship, design, and finish, we may mention the Gold Medals awarded at London, 1862; Paris 1867; Philadelphia, 1876;

THE CARRIAGE YARD

THE CARRIAGE SHOW ROOM

Paris, 1878; Sydney, 1879; Melbourne, 1880; Calcutta, 1884; and 'Inventions,' 1885. Such a record demands no words of commendation, indeed, every word of praise outside the bare facts would be superfluous and distasteful, not more to the reader than the firm to whose achievements the facts testify.

A brief tour of inspection enables us to place succinctly before the public some of the features of interest which entitle the firm to distinguished notice in these pages. The wood-yard is extensive and heavily stocked with well-seasoned English oak, American and English ash, walnut, hickory, elm, birch, mahogany, and other hard woods. The smithy contains ten hearths, equipped with all modern improvements; there are also steam blast, drills, lathes, and every appliance for spring and tyre making. The body and wheel making departments are also busy scenes of activity, but the artistically minded visitor may perhaps take keener interest in the painting department, where may usually be seen the progress of some exquisite specimens of heraldic work, not to mention the always interesting operations of priming, filling, and finishing the vehicles with their numerous coats of paint and varnish.

Throughout the works a perfect system of heating prevails, and, in the varnish rooms especially, there is a remarkable freedom from untidiness and dust. The upholstering and furnishing sections, too, are thoroughly equipped and up-to-date even to the minutest detail.

Messrs. McNaught & Co. also carry on harness manufacture, a branch in which no less creditable results have been attained than in the carriage building department. The showrooms cover an immense area. They are invariably stocked to repletion with specimens of every fashionable class of vehicle, from the Landau or Victoria down to the much required Bath cart or Governess car. The firm have a London depot which caters largely for patrons concerned in state, civic, and ceremonious functions. Messrs. McNaught have supplied the carriage of London's Lord Mayor, and many a Metropolitan and English County Sheriff has drawn upon the resources of this firm for the state equipages essential to the due dignity of their respective offices; and include among their patrons the names of H.R.H.'s the Prince of Wales, and the Duke of Connaught. The firm have branches at No. 10 Park Lane, Piccadilly, London, W., and at 7 and 8 Broad Street, Birmingham. The head of the concern has had a life-long practical experience in the business. He is a member of the Council, and a Past President of the Institute of British Carriage Builders. He is a member of the Coach Maker's Corporation, a member of the Society of Arts, and has filled the onerous, yet decidedly honourable position of Juror of Award at the Edinburgh and the Brussels Exhibitions, respectively. Some idea may be formed from the foregoing sketch of the capacity and industrial capabilities of one of the principal carriage and harness producing establishments in England.

THE BLACKSMITH'S SHOP

MR. JAMES F. WILLIS
Shoe Manufacturer, Worcester

There is no name better known in the boot and shoe trade in the United Kingdom than that of 'Willis of Worcester,' and our review of the industrial resources of the 'Faithful City' would be altogether incomplete were not prominent mention made of so important a factory as that conducted by this eminent firm. The principal of the concern, Mr. James F. Willis, was formerly in partnership with his brother, Mr. Henry Willis, who was the inventor of the process now universally employed for dressing calf-kid. The latter gentleman, however, died about eight years ago, since which time the sole control has remained in the present hands. In 1889, when the business had been in existence for thirty-five years, the heads of the firm were entertained at a dinner, given by their work-people, at the Albion Inn, Bath Road, when it was stated that Messrs. Willis were paying the best wholesale wages in the country. This, we believe, is a fact, and it throws an obvious side-light on the character of the firm's manufactures. From the outset the house has been noted for what are known in the trade as 'best ladies' and childrens';' these are made from the finest qualities of leather obtainable, and it may be mentioned, *inter alia*, that Worcester is a very favourable market for the purchase of such leathers, inasmuch as the city has long constituted a flourishing centre of the glove manufacture, for which, of course, the choicest leathers produced have always to be requisitioned.

The factory occupies a prominent position in Sidbury, in the southern quarter of the city, and close to the cathedral. The main building is a five-story

WILLIS' BOOT FACTORY

elevation, and of considerable depth, and at the rear a further large building is available. The interior has been arranged upon the most convenient lines, being admirably organised throughout, and affording ample facilities for the production of a substantial output.

Originally, the whole of the work was done by hand labour, but of late years, various improved mechanical appliances have been introduced. It should be noted, however, that the management make a point of using machinery only when such machinery can execute certain work in a more efficient style than if it were done in the ordinary way. Hence, it comes to pass that mechanical aid has been a gain to the quality of the firm's specialities, rather than a loss, as is the case in many other factories which might be instanced.

Altogether the works afford employment to about 300 hands. Steam and gas power are utilised for driving the plant, and the whole place is well lighted and ventilated. The goods manufactured are famous throughout the trade as the 'Cinderella' boots and shoes. For perfection of fit, elegance of style, comfort in wear, and great durability, they have yet to be surpassed. The greatest possible care is exercised in their production; close attention is given to details; nothing but the best and choicest materials being used. The 'Cinderella' boots and shoes are made in every size, from the smallest child's to the largest woman's, and in five different fittings and widths of soles. Amongst the more popular shapes we may instance 'Le Printemps,' 'L'Ete,' 'L'Automne,' and 'L'Hiver,' specially adapted, as their names implied, for the various seasons of the year; the 'Park' shoe, the 'Cinderella' slipper, and the 'Times' school boots. Mr. Willis's trade extends to all parts of the United Kingdom; and, latterly, a substantial and steadily increasing export connection has been developed.

MESSRS. J. SIGLEY, SON, & CO.
City Steam Confectionery Works,
Carden Street, Worcester

There are few trades which have shown such remarkable development during recent years as that of the manufacture of confectionery. Thirty or forty years ago, only a very small variety, and those of the commonest kind of sweetmeats, were made in Great Britain, all the better classes being imported. At present our own manufacturers are capable of meeting all the demands of the market, and their productions are justly held in higher repute than those of continental houses.

In Worcester the industry is represented by Messrs. J. Sigley, Son, & Co., whose name is well-known throughout the United Kingdom. This business was founded twenty-five years ago, and has had a career of continuous success, bearing abundant evidence

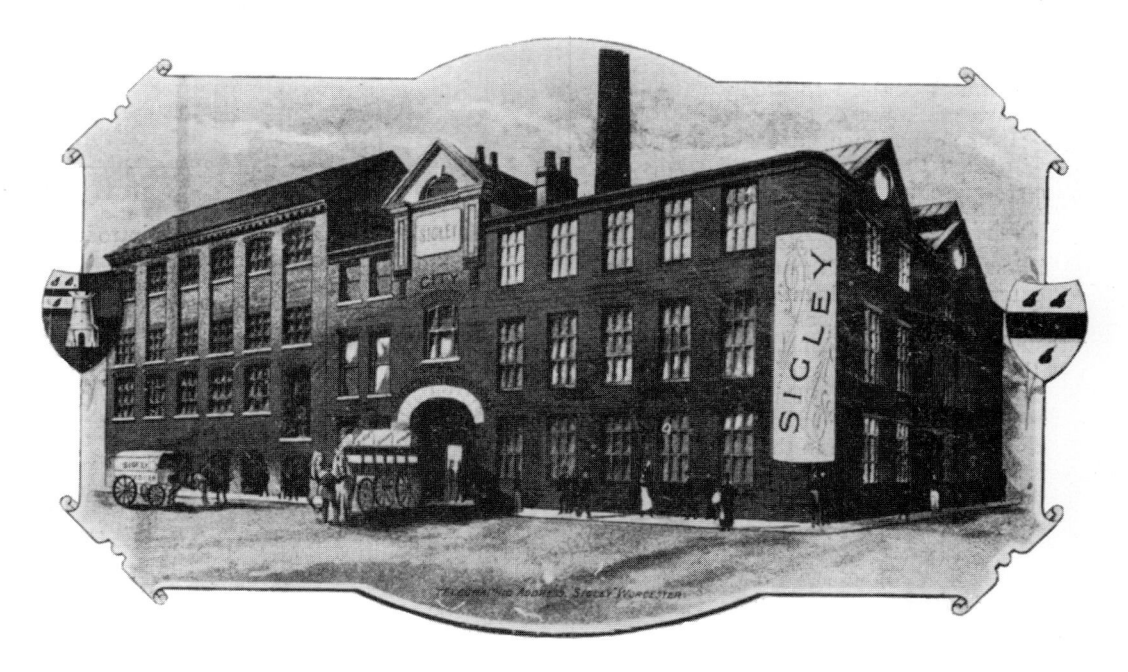

THE CITY STEAM CONFECTIONERY WORKS

of the energetic and enterprising principles adopted in its management.

The City Steam Confectionery Works are very centrally situated in Carden Street, where they cover a considerable area of ground. Besides the factory, which is one of the best equipped concerns of the kind in the country, the firm have branch depots in Broad Street, High Street, and Friar Street. By the courtesy of the proprietors we were privileged to make a tour of the premises, and were particularly struck with their scrupulous cleanliness and by the perfect sanitary conditions under which all operations are carried on. As to the purity of the confectionery produced, we may state that the firm have reports of public analysts all testifying to the wholesomeness of the ingredients they use.

About two hundred hands are employed, and the manufacturing plant is as complete as modern engineering skill can render it. Messrs. Sigley & Co. manufacture all kinds of sweets. These are all the choicest flavours and command a ready sale wherever they are introduced. A speciality is made of the Cough Drops, prepared by Mother Sigley. The firm are constantly introducing novelties of the choicest description, and among their latest introductions must be mentioned the manufacture of chocolate, for which they have just laid down new plant and machinery. The chocolate manufactured by Messrs. Sigley will be pure and good as their other productions, and will undoubtedly command a large sale. Several travellers represent the house among their numerous customers in all parts of the country, and valuable export orders are frequently received.

Mr. John Sigley, the founder and senior member of the firm, is a gentlemen held in the highest esteem in Worcester, and is a valuable member of the City Council, representing the Ward of All Saints.

PEMBERTON & SON
Brush Manufacturers, Broad Street, Worcester

Among the industries of Worcester the manufacture of brushes holds a very prominent position, and the well-known firm of Pemberton & Son, take the lead in this line. The business is one of the oldest existing in the 'Faithful City,' dating back, as it does, over a period of 120 years.

The firm's showrooms should be inspected by every visitor to Worcester. The works, which are situate in Blackfriars, also merit notice as being the centre of active operations, giving employment to a staff numbering about 120 hands. Within the warehouse an enormous stock is held. The works, too, are of considerable dimensions, and are admirably fitted up with every useful accessory and labour-saving contrivance. Messrs. Pemberton & Son employ only the best materials, and every care is taken to turn out a genuinely reliable article. The firm manufacture every conceivable description of brush, and their handsomely bound and copiously illustrated catalogue is a triumph of comprehensiveness and completeness in detail.

The newly erected factory having been furnished throughout with an excellent equipment of the latest and most improved machinery, the firm is enabled to produce the best possible article at a minimum of cost. The Messrs. Pemberton's long experience and unsurpassed facilities enable them to compete on advantageous terms with any house in the trade, whether home or export. Several travellers represent the house and cover the whole of the Midlands, the Western Counties and South Wales, in all parts of which the firm have extensive and influential connections. Messrs. Pemberton give their best attention to all orders entrusted to them, and constantly endeavour to maintain their reputation for excellence of manufacture, which earned for them a Prize Medal at the Great International Exhibition of 1862, and also unqualified expressions of praise in the official report of the Worcestershire Exhibition of 1882.

We may add that the firm's Telegraphic address is, 'Pemberton, Worcester.'

MESSRS. FRENCH & BOYCE,
Boot and Shoe Manufacturers, Worcester

Worcester has long been noted for the production of the fine classes of leather, and the city is, therefore, admirably adapted for the site of a factory such as that of Messrs. French & Boyce, who successfully aim at the production of as dainty coverings for the feet as some of their neighbours do for the hands.

The business was founded as far back as 1820; and during the three-quarters of a century that it has been in existence, the firm have consistently maintained the highest reputation alike for the excellence of their manufactures and for their straightforward and honourable methods of trading. The factory, which is situated in Foregate Street, is very extensive, and is admirably adapted to the requirements of the trade. That the firm keep abreast of the times is shown in the completeness of their manufacturing facilities which they have at command. The plant includes the expensive and complicated 'Goodyear' machinery, which imitates hand-sewn work to perfection, at greatly reduced cost. At the same time, hand-sewn goods of the highest quality are also produced. A large number of skilled hands are employed, and the out-put of finished goods from the factory reaches very considerable figures. Messrs. French & Boyce have invented and introduced to the market several important specialties which deservedly enjoy the highest reputation wherever they are known. Among these may be mentioned the very appropriately named 'Luxurious' seamless button and lace boots, and shoes made on 'Anatomical' principles. These latter have been warmly recommended for their hygienic qualities by Dr. Strange

THE MANUFACTURY

(President of the British Medical Association, 1883), who described them as the *'Beau Ideal'* of Hygienic footwear.

Although the firm make excellence of workmanship and quality their first consideration, their long experience, and the splendid facilities which they have at command, enable them to compete in price with any house in the trade, manufacturing high-class boots and shoes. That this fact is fully appreciated by dealers and the public, the steady growth of the business bears abundant evidence. In 1890 Mr. John French retired, and the present sole proprietor is Mr. Thomas Boyce, who is a gentleman occupying a prominent position in social and commercial circles in Worcester. The esteem in which he is held was evinced by his election, last November, to the City Council, without opposition.

MESSRS. MELLOR & CO.
Sauce Manufacturers, Severn Bridge, Worcester

PROPRIETORS AND MANUFACTURERS OF THE CELEBRATED 'MELLOR'S SAUCE'

No more popular features of table equipment can be suggested than those which bear the familiar green and red labels of Messrs. Mellor & Co., whose celebrated condiments find a place in the great majority of establishments dedicated to purposes of refreshment, whether club, hotel, restaurant, or habitation of civilised mankind, both at home and abroad. The firm has been established for over thirty years as manufacturers of the delicious relish which has, perhaps, a wider circulation than any other of the numerous preparations, often of inferior quality, with which the market is flooded.

Some indication of the extent of Messrs. Mellor & Co.'s business is furnished by the magnitude of their premises, situated on the banks of the Severn, of which the buildings constitute a conspicuous landmark. The principal block has a commanding elevation of four storeys, with extensive frontage to Bridge Street, close to the Severn bridge, and here are placed the handsome and commodious general and private offices, warehouse, and stores for bottled goods ready for transmission. An adjoining building faces the river on one side, where there is wharfage accommodation for the barges used in conveying packages of sauces, and a railway siding running direct into the premises provides further facilities for carriage to all parts of the United Kingdom. The manufactory is replete with all the requisite plant and machinery for grinding and preparing the various ingredients, which for obvious reasons may not be described, but are invariably of the highest quality.

About one hundred male and female hands are employed in the several departments in the preparation, bottling, labelling, and packing the sauces, the whole of which are carried out on well organised methods, and under conditions of the most scrupulous cleanliness and perfect sanitation. The specialities for which Messrs. Mellor & Co. are noted are their 'Piquant' and 'Mild' sauces, the first being embellished with green, and the latter with red labels, and their 'Crown Relish.' All of these are excellent accompaniments to meats, fish, entrées, gravies, soups, etc., and have been highly approved by gastronomic experts for their delicious and appetising properties, and are equally commended for absolute purity, flavour, and digestive qualities. These articles are supplied by grocers and Italian warehousemen of repute in every town and village in the United Kingdom, and are in use in the principal clubs, hotels, etc., in the country. A large and steadily increasing trade is also done in the export markets, heavy shipments of these sauces being forwarded to New Zealand, Australia, South Africa, South America, and British Columbia; Mellor's sauces, indeed, 'following the flat' in every direction where civilisation progresses. The firm's shipping depot in London is at 29, Gracechurch Street, E.C., from whence the chief shipping houses are supplied.

MESSRS. MELLOR & CO'S SAUCE WORKS

MESSRS. BAYLIS, LEWIS & CO.

Manufacturers of Artistic and Unique Fancy Stationery, including Office and Pocket Calendars, Memorial Cards, Fancy Bordered Cards, Menu Cards, Christmas Cards, Ball Programmes, Embossed Circular Borders in Gold and Colour, Poster and other Borders, Fancy Silver and Gold Edged Cards, etc., and Fancy Decorated Notepaper with plain and gilt edges.

The comprehensive list of manufactures embodied in the above heading indicates the principal lines of the extensive business of Messrs. Baylis, Lewis & Co., which also includes other departments of a more ordinary and everyday character, such as commercial letterpress and lithographic printing, envelope making, relief and plain stamping, box making, machine ruling, and the manufacture of account books, &c.

The firm has been established for upwards of fifty years, but it is within the last dozen years that it has been successfully developed into the largest concern devoted to the manufacture of

THE OFFICES AND WORKS OF MESSRS BAYLIS, LEWIS & CO.

artistic and unique stationery, etc., in the Midland Counties, in fact, it may be said that it is the only firm carrying on the manufacture of such high-class and unique goods in the Midland Counties.

Behind the old-fashioned and decidedly unpretentious frontage are a number of workshops in which a large staff of workpeople are employed carrying out the various processes of manufacture; and in addition to this is the large printing works on the ground floor level, a portion of which is illustrated on the previous page. The latter portion of the premises is admirably adapted for the purpose, well lighted from the roof, from the north only, which is so essential where chromo-lithography of a high-class and delicate nature has to be carried on, and fully equipped with all the latest improvements in plant, and appliances for the production of the highest quality of artistic work in lithographic and letter press printing, etc.

Machinery, including American, German and French, besides some of the best machinery made in this country, is here in use. Their productions are distributed throughout Great Britain and Ireland, the British Colonies, and on the Continent, in fact, to nearly all parts of the world, through the agency of some of the largest paper manufacturers and wholesale stationers, whose travellers carry sample books showing a large array of patterns of the various classes of goods, and sell the same to printers and stationers, as before stated, not only throughout the British Isles, but in the Colonies and on the Continent. At their depot, St. Bride Street, London, they hold a representative stock to facilitate supplying the wants of printers in London, and country orders received daily by the various London firms whose travellers are scattered throughout the Kingdom.

Instead of contenting themselves with entering the lists against the ordinary provincial printer they compete with some of the oldest and finest printers in the Kingdom with complete success. In short, this firm has purely by the merits and excellence of its productions made a reputation second to none in its particular line.

MESSRS. R. SMITH & CO.
Brush Manufacturers, 41 High Street, Worcester

There are few better known names in the Brush trade than that of Messrs. Smith & Company, of Worcester, whose reputation for turning out the best classes of goods is unrivalled. The business was founded in 1797, so that this year it will celebrate its centenary; and the firm have every reason to be proud of so long and honourable a record. The present proprietors of the business are Messrs. T. W. and E. P. Davies, who have now carried it on for nearly forty years, with ever-increasing success. The firm's premises are centrally situated in High Street, near the Market and the Guildhall. They comprise a substantial building, of striking appearance, which has been recently entirely re-fitted, and lighted by electricity.

The works, which are at the rear, are equipped with the latest and most improved machinery and labour saving appliances adapted to the requirements of the trade, motive power being derived from a fine gas engine of modern construction. Upwards of a hundred hands are kept constantly employed, and the output of manufactured articles reaches very remarkable quantities. Messrs. Smith & Company are widely known for their capital series of registered brooms and brushes for the protection of furniture. These are made in all shapes, and for all purposes, but each has the special equipment which renders this design so valuable. This consists of padded cushions of velvet at the ends for the protection of anything the brush may be knocked against - whether furniture, or the paint on doors and skirtings of the rooms. These brushes have been most favourably reviewed in the trade journals; and are in great demand wherever a superior article is required.

Travellers represent the firm in most of the principal towns, and an export trade is carried on, chiefly with the Cape and Australia. This business constitutes one of the old standard industrial institutions of Worcester, and is one of which the city may well be proud. We may add that Messrs. Smith & Company are pleased to supply their illustrated wholesale price list on application. Established 1797.

THE PREMISES OF MESSRS. R. SMITH & CO.

NICHOLSON & SON
Organ Builders, Palace Yard, Worcester

The ancient and profoundly interesting craft of organ building has in Worcester been brought to the highest state of perfection by the above-mentioned firm, which for the past half-century and more has exemplified the highest achievements of an art that nowhere out of England has received more judicious exposition or called forth more intelligent application or truly artistic and scientific principles. The very profession and calling of the organ builder suggests what Milton has styled 'thoughts ecclesiastical' and it seems quite in accordance with the eternal fitness of things that Messrs. Nicholson & Co.'s extensive factory should nestle under the very shadow of the glorious cathedral which for ages has fostered the love of music, while employing the very 'king of instruments' to set forth the reverent praises of the Infinite within its venerable walls. Messrs. Nicholson & Co. date their business from the year 1841, and the history of the concern has been one unbroken record of successful enterprise.

The business commenced in a modest manner, and even when it was found necessary to secure more extensive premises in Palace Yard, the factory premises were comparatively insignificant when viewed in the light of present day actualities. From time to time the works have been enlarged to meet growing needs, until now the establishment presents an aspect of completeness that few metropolitan and hardly any

A NICHOLSON ORGAN IN THE CITY HALL, WORCESTER

provincial organ building factories can surpass. Here a large number of workmen are employed, all of them expert craftsmen in their several departments, and, with the assistance of the most effective machinery and appliances that practical experience can devise and suggest, every process in the building of pipe organs is systematically carried out under the most favourable conditions.

The factory is so self-contained that every process is carried on under the closest managerial supervision. Even the pipes are cast and modelled on the premises while the stock of well seasoned timber held represents many hundreds of pounds in value. An artistic spirit pervades all Messrs. Nicholson's work, and their instruments prove beyond all question that their first aim is to secure true musical quality of tone, perfect mechanism and workmanship. Forced and noisy tones are unknown in the firm's organs, but instead, we find a pure mellow diapason-like body of sound that is the glory of Father Smith's and other great typical instruments.

Messrs. Nicholson carry indisputable credentials in the notable array of fine organs they have built and erected at home and abroad. These instruments are found in England and at the most distant parts of the globe, and the satisfaction they give is the best possible tribute to the *bona fides* of their makers. The organ in the Public Hall, Worcester, is one of the finest in the kingdom and consists of 4-manuals, full pedal organ and 59 stops. It contains 2882 sounding pipes, pneumatic lever action to great and swell manuals, and the bellows are blown by two hydraulic engines. This is the third organ the firm have built for the Public Hall, Worcester. Another very fine 4-manual instrument erected by the firm in The Priory Church, Great Malvern, has been much admired by organists and other visitors to that delightful health resort.

Had our space permitted we might have supplied a long list, not only of notable achievements, but of no less convincing testimonials from the greatest organists of this country who speak to the faithful manner in which Messrs. Nicholson & Co., carry out their contracts. The head of the concern is a gentleman of high executive as well as technical ability, and he is capably assisted in the management by Mr. John Waldron, a gentleman who has spent something over half a century in connection with the business.

MR. E. J. OLDS
Wholesale Boot and Shoe Manufacturer, Worcester

Although Worcester does not approach Leicester and Northampton in the extent of their productions in the boot and shoe trade, what the 'Faithful City' lacks in the quantity it more than makes up for in the quality of the goods manufactured. This ancient town on the Severn has for generations been noted for the production of the best classes of foot-gear on the market, and its reputation in this department is not even second to its fame in the kindred glove trade.

Among the names most intimately associated with this industry special mention is due to that of Mr. E. J. Olds, whose 'Arboretum' BRAND of boots and shoes is known throughout the United Kingdom, and held in the highest estimation wherever it is introduced. The 'ARBORETUM' Boot Works are very centrally situated in that part of the city called the Arboretum. One of the leading features of this house is its department for Specials, which receive immediate attention and despatch. Mr. Olds gives personal attention, being well acquainted with the particular requirements of the bespoke trade, has commanded considerable success. The great bulk of the work is done by hand, thus ensuring the best results. Indeed, in these days of shoddy and machine-made boots and shoes, which are simply produced to sell, and not to wear, it is gratifying to encounter such an establishment as this, where quality is made the first consideration. Mr. E. J. Olds manufactures exclusively high-class boots and shoes, and produces the most elegant results, satisfying the most refined taste, at the same time guaranteeing durability and comfort. His speciality consists of the solid-edge soled boots and shoes, a method which adds very considerably to the wearing qualities of the goods, without detracting from the lightness and smart appearance. The house has enjoyed an unrivalled reputation for the past twenty years, and Mr. E. J. Olds' goods are sold by leading retailers in every part of the country, and are in great demand wherever they have been tried. All goods bearing the 'Arboretum' BRAND are warranted by the firm to give every satisfaction. The public will do well to enquire for them. No first-class retailer should be without 'THE ARBORETUM BRAND.'

Portrait of a Victorian City 59

THE 'ARBORETUM' BRAND

DENT, ALLCROFT, & CO.
Glove Manufacturers, Worcester

The antiquity of the glove as an article of human adornment is unquestionable. Records exist among the Greeks and Persians showing that for fully a thousand years before Christ - in the Trojan games, in fact - mailed gauntlets were used either as weapons of offence or tokens of defiance, while the skins of the kids of goats were put upon the hands so early as in the days of Esau. The cave-men, belonging to a very remote age, also wore gloves, if we are to believe high geological authority. In England, gloves were worn so early as the year A.D. 712; while in France, Charlemagne, in 790, granted permission to hunt deer for the purpose of making gloves. More than one reference is made by Shakespeare to gloves; while later writers, of course, need not be quoted. The glove industry is the most ancient in Worcester, the Glover's Company here dating back to the year 1497.

The industry is still the most important one in the city, and at the head of the many establishments devoted to the production of these articles must undoubtedly be ranked the world-renowned firm of Dent, Allcroft & Co., who also carry on extensive establishments at London, Leicester, Torrington, Martock, Paris, Prague, Halberstadt, Grenoble, Brussels, Leipzic, Ottignes, New York, and Naples. The business is one of considerable antiquity, and its development has been astounding.

The premises in Worcester occupy a considerable area, and stand on the east bank of the river Severn, in close proximity to the Cathedral and the ancient Episcopal Palace. The works were in former times the residential mansion of the well-known Warmstry family, and in this connection had space permitted, much interesting historical gossip might have been introduced into this necessarily brief sketch. The firm manufacture every description of leather glove, including those made from the skin of the goat, the kid, chevrette, reindeer, sheep, calf, and colt. The processes carried on embrace every operation involved, from the dressing of the raw skin to the subsequent dyeing and conversion into gloves. Some idea of the magnitude of the firm's operations may be formed from the fact that about 1000 hands are regularly employed in the works, while a large number of women carry on the art of glove making for the house at their respective homes. Of the personal esteem in which the principals have always been held, it is needless to speak, for the name has become a household word throughout the 'Faithful City.' Our claim to publishing a representative work is undoubtedly strengthened by the fact of a house of such great industrial and commercial significance figuring in its pages.

DENT'S GLOVE FACTORY

THE BELL HOTEL
Family and Commercial Hotel, Broad Street, Worcester
Proprietor: Mr. Frank Williams

This is an age of hotel enterprise; but one cannot help feeling that what many of our hostelries are gaining in elegance, they are rapidly losing in comfort. The hotels of the good old-fashioned type, where, like Falstaff, one 'may take his ease,' are fast disappearing to make room for huge *caravanserai*, where the visitor loses his identity, and becomes known, like a convict, by his number, and where cold formality has taken the place of the hearty welcome which at one time formed so pleasing a feature of the English inn. There are, however, a few of the establishments of the good-old sort remaining, among which a very honourable place is

THE BELL HOTEL

occupied by the 'Bell' at Worcester, which combines old-world comfort with the refinements and conveniences of modern life.

The 'Bell' is, we believe, the oldest hotel in Worcester, and flourished mightily in the days 'ere George Stephenson's great invention revolutionised our methods of locomotion. Unlike many an old coaching-house, the 'Bell' has adapted itself to modern requirements, and is as great a favourite with the travelling public to-day as it was when the sound of the post-horn was heard outside its door. The hotel is very conveniently situated between the Cross and Severn Bridge, and the building, in its solidity, seems to give some warrant of the substantial comforts to be obtained within.

The interior is very commodious, and is lighted throughout by electricity, on the incandescent principle. There are very comfortable bars and bar parlour; elegantly-furnished coffee and commercial rooms; a quiet reading-room combined; several excellent private sitting-rooms; and about thirty lofty and well-ventilated sleeping apartments, all furnished in that comfortable style which invites repose. Mention should not be omitted of the fine billiard-room, nor of the spacious stock rooms, which render the 'Bell' the favourite house among commercial men.

The culinary arrangements are perfect, and a capital menu, embracing every delicacy in season, is arranged daily. The wines, spirits, and malt liquors are all of the best, and many rare vintages are stored in the cellars. The servants are all well trained, and the attendance is prompt and courteous. Indeed, we know of no more desirable house for visitors to Worcester, be they on business or on pleasure bent. The premises extend through to Angel Street, where are the stables. Here a fine stud of horses are maintained, while vehicles are kept for all purposes. A very good business is carried on in posting in all its branches. The Tariff, in all departments, will be found exceptionally moderate. The hotel is the property of Messrs. W. E. & Frank Williams, the latter gentleman being the resident proprietor; and to his unfailing courtesy and energy not a little of the conspicuous success of the establishment is due.

THE SARACEN'S HEAD HOTEL
The Tything, Worcester
Mr. W. Roberts, Proprietor

The Saracen's Head Hotel, at Worcester, belongs to a type of hostelry which is unfortunately fast disappearing. It is, in fact, one of those of the good old-fashioned, comfortable style, where a man may literally take his ease, without feeling that ease and his surroundings are incompatible. Comfort is the key-note of the whole establishment, and has not been vanished, as in the average modern hotel, to make room for elegance. At the same time the Saracen's Head is provided with all the refinements of modern life, and is furnished in a style conducive to comfort; the sanitary arrangements have been modernised in every particular. The hotel is very conveniently situated in the Tything, not far from Foregate Street Station, and is very handy for those who may have business at the Law Courts.

The visitor on pleasure bent will find it an equally desirable resting-place; and when the yeomanry are up, this house constitutes their headquarters. The cooking leaves nothing to be desired, and a most liberal table is provided. The dining room on the ground floor is a spacious and lofty apartment capable of accommodating 150 guests, as seen in the picture on the next page. During the sitting of the Quarter Sessions and Assizes, an ordinary is daily provided for, and accommodation of those engaged at the Courts, and the room is available during the summer months for Bean feasts and pleasure parties, the accommodation being specially adapted for that business.

The hotel is particularly noted for its splendid home-brewed ales, and also for its wines and spirits which are all of excellent quality, thoroughly matured. There is excellent stabling attached to the house, and posting arrangements are made. There is also capital accommodation for cyclists, among whom the hotel is very popular.

The proprietor is, Mr. W. Roberts, who is a most genial host, and spares no pains to insure the comfort of this guests.

Portrait of a Victorian City 65

THE DINING ROOM, THE SARACEN'S HEAD HOTEL

LEWIS, CLARKE, & CO.
Brewers, Worcester

Among the descriptions of the various representative businesses of Worcester, we must include the brewery of Messrs. Lewis, Clarke & Co., to which the writer paid a very pleasant visit a short time ago. The brewery, which is well-known to every resident of Worcester, is situated in the heart of the city, at the bottom of Angel Street. The buildings form a compact block, surmounted by a tower, in which, as will be seen, a not unimportant part of the brewing process is carried on. On my request, the firm at once with great courtesy assented to my being shown over the brewery, and I was immediately introduced by that gentleman to the brewer who kindly showed me over. To see the whole process of brewing I was taken first to the upper storey of the tower. Here was shown the hot liquor tun, where the water or mixing is first heated. Adjoining are the grist cases supplying the ground malt which is brought up by a Jacob's ladder, after being ground in the mill below. The malt and the hot water from the

THE BREWERY

adjoining hot liquor tun are from these two sources carried into Steele's Patent Mashers, where they are thoroughly mixed, and from thence discharged into the mash tubs situated in a room immediately beneath. After standing for about two hours in the mash tubs, the wort by means of a false bottom, is run off into the coppers situate in another chamber below, where the hops are added and the whole boiled up together. The next process takes us to the most interesting part of the brewery, consisting of a new building of great size, lined with white enamelled bricks, the whole conveying the idea of the most perfect cleanliness, in fact, more resembling in this respect, a well-ordered dairy than a brewery. Here the wort, after the processes before described, passes over, and is cooled by the splendid refrigerator, and from thence into the large tuns standing on this floor. It is here that the fermentation is begun. On the next floor in the skimming room where the attemperating is done, each vat being fitted with hot and cold water supply, and with a machine for skimming, called a 'parachute.'

COOPERAGE AND CASK WASHING SHED

We now descend to the ground floor, where we find the racking room where the beer is run into casks, which are then turned into the cellar below. Some idea of the size of the big beer cellar may be obtained from the fact that it easily holds one thousand barrels. The casks are raised, when the beer is matured and ready for use, by special machinery. The big engine that works the pumps and other machinery, was duly inspected, together with the cooperage and the patent cask washing machine. The extensive wine cellarage and spirit room, together with several of the private apartments assigned to the brewer and other officials, are situate within the comfortable house which contain Messrs. Lewis, Clarke, & Co's offices.

I finished my visit by the inspection of the well-appointed stabling, and made the acquaintance of 'Diamond' and 'Jubilee,' a pair of the fine draught horses belonging to the firm. What must strike any visitor to Messrs. Lewis, Clarke, & Co's. Brewery is the brightness and spotless cleanliness of all parts of the premises. It is needless to say that the firm transact a large and increasing business, their beers being very popular in the neighbourhood and country around. In the wine department they have in stock a fine selection of vintage ports and champagnes; their clarets, sherries, burgundies, and other wines are of the best brands. So the wayfarer in the district hails the name of Lewis, Clarke, & Co. upon the wayside inn as assuring a good glass of beer and comfortable accommodation. I may add that the firm are always pleased for visitors to Worcester to inspect their brewery, which is, undoubtedly, a model of its kind.

A CONSIGNMENT OF CHAMPAGNE

MESSRS. JOSEPH WOOD & SONS,

Builders and Contractors, English and Foreign Timber, Slate and Coal Merchants, Brickmakers, The Butts, Worcester

Some of the largest and most important public and private works carried out in this and other parts of the Midlands have been completed by Messrs. Joseph Wood & Sons, builders and contractors of this city, whose old-established business is one of the most extensive of Worcester industries. Founded nearly a century ago, the firm has made steady and continuous progress, contemporary with the constant development of the district - which it has had no inconsiderable share in promoting, during the lengthened period of its existence.

MESSRS J. WOOD & SONS' PREMISES

The head-quarters of Messrs. J. Wood & Son's business occupy a central and convenient position in the Butts, adjoining the cattle market, the premises covering an area of over 2 acres in extent. There are two large gateway entrances from the street giving admission to the spacious yards in which are erected the buildings occupied by the various industrial departments. The principal of these are the two buildings, of two storey elevation, in which are contained the sawing, planing, and moulding mills. These are equipped with a full complement of modern plant, and appliances for every branch of wood-working, on the most efficient and expeditious lines.

Motive force for the machinery is supplied by a powerful steam engine and boiler erected in a separate structure; the remaining premises comprising offices, stores for materials, and large timber drying sheds. The yard is spanned by a powerful travelling crane, and stacked therein is an immense stock of valuable woods, both home-grown and imported, held to mature until required in the works. The full scope of the firm's business is indicated in the above heading, the most important departments being, perhaps, those in which they undertake the erection of buildings, as per contract.

Among the contracts fulfilled by Messrs. Wood, have been the construction of the noble Victoria Institute, Worcester, one of the finest public libraries and museums in the provinces; the fine building for the Worcester City and County Bank, now amalgamated with Lloyd's Bank, Limited; casemented barracks on Milford Avon; the barracks at Wrexham and other buildings for the War Office and Government, together with many of the principal mansions and private residences in this and the adjoining counties, including Witley Court, the residence of the Rt. Hon. Earl Dudley; 'Impney' Droitwich, the residence of John Corbett, Esq.; mansions for C. W. Lea, Esq., at Worcester, and C. W. D. Perrins, Esq., at Malvern; and, recently, the mansion of Hon. A. P. Allsopp at Battenhall Mount, Worcester.

At Shrub Hill, near the Great Western Railway Goods Station, Messrs. Wood & Sons have extensive brick works, replete with improved plant, and capable of turning out, not only the materials required for their own purpose, but of supplying the requirements of the general trade throughout the district. The firm employ a large number of hands, ranging from two to five hundred, according to the contracts in course of completion, and although the business is on so vast a scale, due attention is paid to the smaller branches of repairing and jobbing work, which are entrusted only to steady and reliable men, and are carried out under the direction of experienced foremen, or one of the principals of the firm.

MESSRS. T. BENNETT & SONS
Photographers, Studios at 8 Broad Street, Worcester and at Malvern

Just over forty years ago, when photography was regarded more as a scientific plaything than as the most wonderful discovery of the age, the firm of Messrs. T. Bennett & Sons, established their studio in the grey old Cathedral city, and commenced practice in taking 'likenesses,' as they were then termed, by the new process of the daguerrotype. During the intervening period what marvellous progress has been made. Improvement has followed improvement with each succeeding decade, and the application of photography to science, art, and industry, may be almost said to have reached its culminating point of development in the discovery of the 'X' Ray, or Röntgen process, which has unfolded the secrets of nature with startling and marvellous effect. Steadily following in the path of progress and improvement, Messrs. T. Bennett & Sons have attained a premier position in their art, and a high professional reputation of far wider than local significance. Their handsome studios, centrally situated at 8 Broad Street, between the Cross and Severn Bridge, present an attractive window frontage utilised for an effective exhibition of artistic specimens of portraits of Royal and distinguished celebrities, views of buildings, and objects of interest in the locality, both architectural and historical. The interior arrangements include reception rooms, replete with every comfort and convenience for sitters awaiting their turn. This apartment is liberally embellished with highly finished pictures by the bromide, carbon, platino-type, and silver point processes, in enlargements, re-produced from original portraits, or smaller copies of photographs, illustrating all the latest improvements in scientific

THE MALVERN PREMISES

photography. The studio proper is a large and splendidly-lighted apartment, completely equipped with all the most recent improvements in apparatus and appliances for the execution of high-class work, from the smallest vignette miniature to the handsome three-quarters or full length presentment of some civic magnate. The accessories provided for taking groups or arranging a suitable background for various styles of pictures desired by sitters, are of the most complete description, enabling the operator to select the details of the surroundings in appropriate harmony with the subject or individual photographed. Thoroughly finished and accomplished experts in the difficult arts of posing and arrangement are retained, and by the aid of the instantaneous process, complete fidelity of expression, and the most natural presentments are obtained in every detail of the portrait. The perfection attained in the case of children's portraits is a noteworthy feature of Messrs. T. Bennett & Son's skilful practice, and another difficult branch of work is specialised in animal and landscape reproduction. In addition to the various departments of photography already indicated, the members of the firm produce some exceedingly well executed oil paintings, both landscape and portrait, which are submitted for inspection at the studios, and evidence the fact that Messrs. Bennett are perfectly competent to hold their own in the higher regions of executive art. The firm have received from time to time flattering recognition of their excellent productions from the highest sources, as evidenced by the following communications:-

THE WORCESTER PREMISES

'BALMORAL.

Sir Henry Ponsonby is commanded by the Queen to thank Messrs. Bennett & Sons for the excellent photographs of the two ceremonies connected with the Worcester Jubilee Statue.'

'SANDRINGHAM,

NORFOLK

Miss Knolly is desired to thank Messrs. Bennett for the photographs they have so kindly forwarded for their Royal Highnesses The Prince and Princess of Wales' acceptance.'

'YORK HOUSE,

ST. JAMES' PALACE, S.W.

Major-General Sir Francis de Winton presents his compliments to Messrs. Bennett & Sons, and is desired by his Royal Highness the Duke of York to thank them for sending the photographs relating to his visit to Worcester, three of which he has kept.'

'YORK HOUSE,

ST. JAMES' PALACE, S.W.

Lady Eva Greville is desired by H.R.H. The Duchess of York to acknowledge receipt of Mr. Bennett's letter, and to thank him most gratefully for the charming Book of Photographs which he has so very kindly sent her. H.R.H. quite well remembers Messrs. Bennett having photographed her on the occasion of her visit to Worcester, and also at the Foley Arms, Malvern.'

'WHITE LODGE,

RICHMOND PARK, SURREY.

SIRS, - I am desired by H.R.H. The Duchess of Teck to return you many thanks for the photographs you have sent, with which Her Royal Highness is much pleased. Yours faithfully -

MARY L. THESIGER.'

    Messrs. Bennett & Sons number among their distinguished circle of patrons, Their Royal Highnesses The Prince and Princess of Wales, and the elite of the nobility, clergy, and resident gentry, both at their Worcester and Malvern establishments.

MESSRS. COOPER & COMPANY

Goldsmiths, Watchmakers, 20, The Cross, Worcester

In the goldsmith's trade in Worcester, there is no difficulty in selecting a house for special mention, for the premier position, in this department, undoubtedly belongs to the establishment of Messrs. Cooper & Company. This business has now been established for many years, and was formerly carried on under the style of D. A. Cooper, & Son, & Co., assuming its present form last July, when Mr. D. A. Cooper retired to enjoy a well-earned rest, and the business is now carried on by his son, Mr. W. Cooper, F.R.A.S.

The firm's premises occupy a prominent site at the corner of the Cross and Angel Street, and have imposing frontages to both those important thoroughfares. The windows have always an attractive display. The interior of the shop is commodious, and very elegantly appointed, and every facility exists for carrying on an extensive high-class trade. Messrs. Cooper & Company hold a large and very valuable stock. Their selection of jewellery is

MESSRS. COOPER & CO'S PREMISES AT THE CROSS

particularly choice, and will be found to include articles in all the best designs. Of silver plate, both modern and antique, they have a magnificent collection, many of the pieces being specially adapted for presentation.

Electro-plated goods, of the best manufacture, are also well represented. The stock also includes a large number of ladies' and gentlemen's gold and silver watches of the finest English and Continental manufacture; marble, ormolu, chime, cuckoo, oak and other clocks and timepieces, aneroid and mercurial barometers and thermometers; opera glasses, spectacles, and other optical goods, bronzes of the best designs, and ormolu and brass goods.

The firm also make a special feature in diamonds and other precious stones. They are also agents for the best Sheffield cutlery. All the above mentioned goods will be found to be chiefly of the best quality, and they are offered at moderate prices, although excellence of quality is never sacrificed to cheapness. Another noteworthy feature about the stock is that everything is thoroughly up-to-date, new goods being constantly introduced, and novelties will be found here as soon as they appear in the best London houses.

Attached to the premises are spacious and well lighted work rooms, equipped with the best machinery and appliances for the manufacture and repairing of watches, clocks, and jewellery. Only thoroughly expert hands are employed in this department, and all orders are executed on the shortest notice. Irreparable damage is often done to delicate pieces of mechanism by sending watches to be repaired by unskilful workmen; but the very highest classes of chronometers may be entrusted to Messrs. Cooper & Company, with perfect confidence. The mean time is telegraphed from Greenwich every week. Messrs. Cooper & Company's house is, in fact, one of the institutions of Worcester, and is certainly a credit to the city.

MESSRS. OSBORNE & SHARPE
Glass, Oil, Lead, and Colour Merchants
St Swithin Street and Trinity Street, Worcester

Our Review of the Commercial resources of Worcester, would be altogether incomplete were mention omitted of the eminent firm whose title heads this brief sketch. Messrs. Osborne & Sharpe established themselves here, about eleven years ago, as Glass, Lead, Oil and Colour Merchants, and speedily secured a very generous measure of support from leading builders plumbers and painters throughout the Midlands. The reason of the firm's rapid success is not far to seek. It lies in the fact that from the first they determined to deal only in the best classes of goods upon the market, and to supply these at the lowest consistent prices. The members of the trades, above referred to, were not slow to recognise these facts, and to show their appreciation of the firms' efforts in a practical manner, so that a substantial business was speedily built up. Messrs. Osborne & Sharpe occupy commodious premises at the corner of St. Swithin and Trinity Street. The offices and retail rooms are in the former, and the wholesale and stock rooms in the latter thoroughfare. The premises were specially erected by the firm in 1895. They consist of handsome red-brick buildings, of three storeys, with basement, affording ample facilities for the storage of vast stocks, and for the reception and despatching of the same.

Both partners are actively engaged in the business and together superintend the whole of their extensive trading operations. The firm deal in Plate, Sheet and Crown Glass; Ornamental, Patent Plate, Rough Rolled, Figured, Rolled and Cast Plate Glass; Glass Slates, Tiles, etc; Silvered Glass and Glass Shades and Louvre Ventilators; Sheet Lead, Lead Pipe, Laminated Lead, Tin, Tin Pipe, Composition Gas Tube. Window Lead, Genuine White Lead, Orange Lead, Red Lead, Leaded Lights; Linseed Oil, Boiled Oil, Turpentine, Putty, Varnishes, Colours of all kind ground in Oil, Patent Dryers, Gold Leaf, Brushes and Painters' Tools, Glue, Size, Glaziers Diamonds, etc., etc; Plumbers' Brass Work, Water Closets, Baths, etc.; Beer Machines, Gas and Steam Fittings, Iron Welded and Galvanized Tubes; Sheet Zinc, Zinc Heads, Gutters, etc.; Cast Iron Spouting and Fittings; Cast Iron Pumps, etc. All these goods are purchased from the best manufacturing houses, and every reliance may be placed upon their excellence of quality. The firm have also a large collection of paper-hangings in the latest and most artistic designs. Estimates in any department are submitted upon application, and from these it will be gathered that the firm's charges are exceptionally moderate.

MESSRS. OSBORNE & SHARPE'S PREMISES

MESSRS. BOWCOTT & COMPANY
Cycle Manufacturers, Dealers, and Repairers,
69, Sidbury, Worcester

Messrs. Bowcott & Company established themselves as Cycle manufacturers, Dealers and Repairers, in Worcester in 1883, when cycling was by no means the fashionable pastime that it is to-day. They now have one of the largest businesses of the kind in this district. The firm's premises are conveniently situated in Sidbury, not far from the cathedral. They comprise a spacious and well appointed show-room, lighted by electricity, with large workshops equipped with the most modern appliances attached; also large stockrooms for display of new and second-hand machines. Messrs. Bowcott & Company have always on hand the largest stock of up-to-date new machines and second-hands in the city. They are sole district representatives for the Rudge-Whitworth, Humber, Raglan, Raleigh, Swift, Osmond, Royal Enfield, Wulfruna, New Howe, Peerless, Riley, Premier, Sparkbrook, and other leading cycles, of

MESSRS. BOWCOTT & CO'S PREMISES IN SIDBURY

which they hold large stocks; and supply all these machines with substantial discounts for cash, or upon easy payments. Old machines are taken in part exchange; and, in this department the business is conducted upon the most equitable terms. The firm have also a large assortment of accessories of the best manufacture, including all the latest novelties. In the operative departments only thoroughly experienced hands are employed, and all classes of repairs, enamelling, painting and lineing and plating are carried out at moderate charges. In this branch orders are executed on the shortest notice, in a style displaying expert and finished workmanship in every detail. The firm have been appointed the official repairers to the Cyclists' Touring Club, and to the Cyclists' Insurance Corporation. Messrs. Bowcott & Company have a very extensive and influential connection in Worcestershire; and are particularly noted for supplying the best ladies' machines on hire, which they will send to any part of the county on most reasonable terms.

A speciality is made of teaching, ladies being taught daily, and proficiency is guaranteed in a very few lessons. Price Lists and terms for teaching may be had upon application. The firm's telegraphic address is, 'Bladder, Sidbury, Worcester,' and orders received through this channel have immediate attention. W. J. Bladder is the managing partner.

J. WHITEHEAD & SON
Tailors and Military Outfitters,
Foregate Street, Worcester

The above mentioned house is justly proud of its very ancient standing as representatives of the sartorial profession in the 'Faithful City,' indeed, the firm is one of the few surviving mercantile institutions in its own line of operations that has withstood the competition of the cheap ready-made clothing merchant. The premises are very centrally situated in the leading thoroughfare of the city, and are near to the General Post Office, the Cross, and the Foregate Street Station. As our illustration shows,

THE PREMISES IN FOREGATE STREET

the shop has a tasteful and a suitable, rather than imposing appearance, there being no attempt at window display. The interior is commodious, extending back over 60 feet, and including, besides the showroom, a comfortable fitting room, cutting department, etc. We need hardly say that the firm hold heavy stocks of the very highest class of woollen cloths, including Scotch Tweeds, West of England wool-dyed Coatings, Cheviots, Serges, Meltons, Vicunas, Diagonals, and other fashionable productions of the loom, all of the latest design and best quality. On the premises are the workshops which are under close personal supervision of the proprietary, and here the sanitary conditions are unexceptionable. The importance of this point cannot be too highly emphasised, as untold evils result too frequently from a careless disregard of hygienic laws in tailoring establishments not properly supervised and indifferently arranged structurally. Every garment produced by the firm will be found to display the perfection of fit, style, finish, and sound workmanship. Special attention is paid to clerical, military, naval and court uniforms, while in the matter of liveries, the house enjoys a reputation not surpassed by that of any West End of London establishment. Indeed, in the matter of liveries, the firm justly prides itself on having secured a connection embracing most of the leading families of the county, and it is gratifying to note that the trade in this department is continuously increasing. The head of the firm, Mr. Christopher John Whitehead, a prominent member of the Town Council of Worcester, has for many years been a churchwarden of St Nicholas parish and a Hop Market guardian. He also holds many other honorary official positions, which unitedly give evidence to the keen interest he takes in the well-being and social advancement of the 'Faithful City.'

MESSRS. W. B. ROWE & SON
Nurserymen, Seedmen, and Florists
Barbourne Nurseries, and 65 Broad Street, Worcester

The science of horticulture, and the improvements in the arts of cultivation and propagation of fruit and forest trees, have never, perhaps, reached a higher stage of development at any period of the world's history than at the present time, when the methods adopted to this end have been perfected to an extent that leaves further advances in this direction an apparent impossibility. This reflection suggests itself as the result of a visit recently paid to the establishment of Messrs. W. B. Rowe & Son, of Worcester, whose extensive business as Nurserymen, Seedsmen, and Florists is the oldest in the county. The business, which has been founded nearly two centuries, was formerly in the possession of Messrs. Wood & Co., from whom it was acquired by the present senior partner, Mr. W. B. Rowe, about thirty years ago. For some time the firm traded

THE NURSERY

under the title of Messrs. W. B. Rowe & Co., Limited, but in November 1896, this style was altered, on Mr. Rowe, Jun., entering into partnership with his father, when the present form was adopted. The seed establishment of the firm is centrally situated at 65 Broad Street, and comprise neat and compact premises with single window, in which is displayed a choice selection of cut flowers, bouquets, wreaths (one of their specialities), seeds, bulbs, and other requisites, of which large and well-assorted stocks are always on hand.

The interior is suitably equipped and appointed, and here may be obtained in addition to the articles already named, all kinds of insecticides, manures, gardeners' sundries, hyacinth glasses, fancy vases and pots, horticultural implements and appliances, which are supplied of best quality at maker's prices. The extensive nurseries at Barbourne are situated one mile from the Cross on the Droitwich Road; tramway cars running from the city in this direction every fifteen minutes. The area occupied covers several acres, a large portion of which is under glass, and appropriated to the propagation of all kinds of flowering plants for garden and decorative purposes. Messrs. Rowe & Son, also make a special feature of supplying hyacinths, tulips, crocuses, and other Dutch flower roots each season, of superior quality, selected with the greatest care from the best growers in Holland. These are made up in large or small parcels to suit all classes of purchasers. The firm are also large growers of fruit trees, roses, shrubs, and plants, well grown, fibrous rooted, and true to name, which are supplied in healthy condition at moderate prices, special quotations being submitted for wholesale quantities.

Messrs. Rowe & Son also undertake landscape gardening in all its branches. The firm number among their patrons the leading nobility and gentry in the country, the list being headed by Her Majesty the Queen and include Lord Windsor, Hewell Park; the Dowager Lady Hindlip, Earl Beauchamp, Lord Hindlip, Lord Sandys, the Hon. Percy Allsopp, and many other influential county families.

MESSRS. J. & N. NADIN & CO
Proprietors of Stanton Collieries, near Burton-on-Trent
Chief Office for Worcester and District, 98, High Street

Exceptional advantages to consumers of fuel, whether for household or factory purposes, are gained by purchasing direct from colliery owners like Messrs. J. & N. Nadin & Co., than by obtaining their supplies from firms who are simply agents, and who thus represent the system of dealing with the 'middle man,' implying, in the generality of cases, an intermediate profit to be paid by the customer. The firm in question is one of the oldest in the trade, the business having been originally established in 1770, a period covering to a remarkable extent the industrial and commercial progress of the Midlands, where the bulk of Messrs. Nadin's colliery products is distributed through their numerous branches. Not the least important of these is that at Worcester, which forms the base of supply for a very large area of the surrounding district. The head-offices in the city are centrally

THE HIGH STREET OFFICES

situated at No. 98, High Street, close to the Cathedral and Guildhall; the branch being under the direction of Mr. Job Whirledge, a gentleman, who for twenty years has represented the firm as manager of this locality.

The Worcester Depot is at the Midland Railway Station, in direct communication with Messrs. Nadin's Stanton Collieries, near Burton-on-Trent, and here spacious accommodation is provided for the large stocks of coal held to meet the current requirements of their extensive connections. Other depots have been established at Bromsgrove, Malvern and Pershore, Bransford and Bromyard, each of these branches being a centre of a large and increasing trade in the neighbourhoods named. Messrs. Nadin & Co. are also factors of all classes of coals from Staffordshire, Warwickshire and Derbyshire collieries, to meet every requirement, and also supply smokeless and anthracite coals for steam users, quotations for which are supplied at the lowest market prices current.

Within the past few years the firm have introduced their 'Special Patent Fuel;' for the preparation of which they have, to a very large extent, perfected their new machinery, erected at the collieries. The Patent Fuel is made of the screenings from the best coals, and by a patent process is compressed into blocks which really surpass coal for hardness and economy in burning; and for drawing room, sitting rooms, and bedrooms is unequalled, as it burns gently and clean, gives out a good heat, and throws no sparks or flyers, thus obviating the risk of fire; it is also very free from dust, making but a very small quantity of dull-brown ash, and as it is easily stored, it forms a most convenient form of fuel for offices and other business places where room is an object. The new fuel has made rapid progress in popular favour with all who have given it a trial, and is unquestionably both cheaper and more convenient than coals for the purposes specified.

The business is thoroughly well-organised in each department, a numerous staff of hands, and several vehicles and horses being employed in the work of delivering orders, which, needless to add, receive the promptest attention from the local manager.

THE AMERICAN DENTISTS' ASSOCIATION
Messrs. Bradlaw, Phillips & Company,
1, Angel Street, Worcester

The superiority of the American system of dentistry over all others has been amply demonstrated during the past two decades; and the remarkable success achieved by the American Dentists' Association (Messrs. Bradlaw, Phillips & Company), in this country, proves that the British public fully appreciate this fact. Not many years ago, a visit to the dentists was viewed by all with apprehension, if not with actual horror; and it is due to our American cousins that this has been all changed, and that one can enter the dental surgery with as little fear as one would a hairdressing saloon.

By the American system there is no need to extract teeth, and it is consequently painless. Then the most useless stumps and shells of teeth are utilised as the bases of crowns, which make them perfect for masticating; while the artificial teeth supplied by the Association are made with such skill as to defy detection. At the same time the charges are about half those demanded by other dentists, who are vainly trying to keep up a monopoly at the expense of the public. Space precludes our giving any detailed account of this admirable system of dentistry, but full particulars will be found in the capital little brochure issued by the Association, which should be in the hands of every sufferer from dental afflictions. Messrs. Bradlaw, Phillips and Company have an establishment in Worcester, centrally situated at the corner of the Cross and Angel Street, and having an entrance in the latter throughfare. There are several comfortable reception rooms, operating rooms, equipped with the most modern appliances, and large workshops, where all mechanical processes are carried through. This establishment has been opened since 1889, and has gained the confidence and support of all sections of the community.

THE PREMISES

MR. WALTER LEE
Hatter, Hosier, Glover, 79 High Street, Worcester

Among gentlemen residing in Worcester and district, no establishment in the gentlemen's out-fitting trade enjoys a higher reputation than that of Mr. Walter Lee. This well-known business was founded over 70 years ago by Mr. Chaplain, and was afterwards carried on by Mr. Albert Wilks, from whom it was acquired by the present proprietor, who has more than maintained the high reputation which the house has so long enjoyed, and has extended its connections in all directions.

The premises which are conveniently situated in High Street, comprise a particularly neat shop, the windows of which are always dressed in the most tasteful style. The interior is commodious and admirably appointed, with well-arranged work-rooms attached. Particular attention is devoted to the making of shirts and collars to order; and in this direction the production of the house are unrivalled in the city.

The stock includes silk and felt hats and caps by the most famous manufacturers, the choicest hosiery, gloves of all kinds, a particularly fine selection of fashionable ties, umbrellas, portmanteaus and handbags, rugs and driving aprons, dressing gowns, water-proofs etc., etc. All these articles will be found of the best quality, and are offered at exceptionally moderate prices. Indeed, we doubt if any other house in the county offers so wide a choice to customers, and certainly there is none where one can get better value. The business is admirably managed, and reflects great credit upon its enterprising proprietor.

MR. LEE'S SHOP

MESSRS. BROMAGE & EVANS
Builders and Contractors,
Derby Road, and London Road, Worcester

In a review of this description the building trades call for special attention, and in this department we can choose no more representative house in Worcester than that of Messrs. Bromage & Evans. The business conducted by this enterprising firm was founded a quarter of a century go, and has had a career of remarkable success. The yard and workshops are situated in Derby Road, on the Worcester and Birmingham Canal. The works are thus brought into communication by water carriage with the industrial centres of the Midlands, and with the ports on the Bristol Channel, thus affording excellent facilities for transport purposes. The works and yard cover an area of an acre. The wood-working plant is particularly complete, including circular, horizontal and band saws, lathes, morticing, planing, moulding and other machines, and mortar mill, all driven by steam power.

THE BUILDERS' WORKS

Large stocks of building materials of all kinds are kept, including sanitary appliances of the most modern kind, the firm being noted for the excellence of their work as plumbers. Messrs. Bromage & Evans's head offices are situated in Sidbury, opposite to Bath Road, and are interesting from the fact that they were once occupied by Brock, the famous sculptor and Royal Academician. Figures carved by him still surmount the door and windows. The firm are prepared to estimate for any class of building operations; and in all cases they carry out orders on the shortest notice, in a style displaying expert and finished workmanship in every detail. They have erected a large amount of excellent residential property in and around Worcester, and are also noted as builders of schools. Most of these establishments in Worcester have been erected by them, including the British schools, St. Martin's Gate School, St. Peter's School, and the Hindlip schools for Lord Hindlip, and shop fronts and fittings for the majority of the best known Houses in Worcester.

The business is admirably managed and organised, and reflects the highest credit upon its proprietors. Messrs. Bromage & Evans also carried out a very interesting piece of work in removing the Old Trinity House from the position it had occupied for over 400 years to its present site. This old house, from the balcony of which Queen Elizabeth is said to have addressed the citizens of Worcester, was saved from demolition by the action of some of the citizens, and was removed by Messrs. Bromage & Evans some considerable distance. The great engineering skill and perseverance displayed by the firm in this matter has gained them a deservedly high position in their business, and in the estimation of their fellow citizens.

MESSRS. BULFORD & MADELEY
Provision Merchants
10, Mealcheapen Street, Worcester

In reviewing the leading business houses of Worcester, one cannot fail to be impressed by the remarkable longevity which many of them display. This fact need, however, excite no surprise when we remember what a long and prosperous career the 'Faithful City' has enjoyed. Unlike the mushroom towns which have sprung up to the north of it, with Birmingham as a centre, Worcester was esteemed a place of importance centuries ago; and the city entertained kings and princes when the names of many leading industrial towns of the present day had no place on the maps of the country. A notable example of one of these houses is afforded by the establishment of Messrs. Bulford and Madeley, whose business was founded as far back as 1752. The firm have by them some very curious orders, which throw some light upon the cost of house-keeping during the last century. Old as the business is, it is now conducted upon thoroughly modern principles, and with energy and enterprise, which promise it as long a future as it has had a past.

THE PREMISES IN MEALCHEAPEN STREET

The premises are situated in Mealcheapen Street, and have a somewhat quaint appearance, although they are lighted by electricity. There is a commodious shop, with ample storage space attached, and well-arranged offices at the rear. Messrs. Bulford and Madeley hold large and well-selected stocks of the best classes of provisions, including hams, bacon, cheese, lard, butter, eggs, etc. These are purchased direct from the best markets, and while they will be found of very superior quality, are offered at exceptionally moderate prices. Indeed, excellence and cheapness are the leading characteristics of this establishment.

The trade is wholesale and retail, and extends throughout Worcester, and for many miles round the city.

MESSRS. G. W. Y. LEWIS & SON
Wholesale Commercial and Fancy Stationers
69, Broad Street, Worcester

One of the oldest businesses in Worcester is that conducted by Messrs. G. W. Y. Lewis & Son, the well-known wholesale stationers which was founded as far back as 1750. It has always been in the hands of the same family, which is one of the most respected in the city. The present representative, and sole proprietor of the business, is Mr. W. G. Lewis, who conducts all his affairs upon the

THE BROAD STREET POST OFFICE

most modern principle, and has succeeded in extending the trade of the house in all directions. The premises are very centrally situated in Broad Street, near the Cross, the Station, etc. The shop, which has a double frontage, is well adapted to the requirements of the extensive trade in operation.

Eight years ago it became the Broad Street Post Office, and is fitted for this purpose. The firm hold very large and well-selected stock, their selections of commercial and fancy stationery being probably the largest and most comprehensive in the city. Every requisite for the office, school-room, and study will be found included. We also noted beautifully bound Bibles, Church services, and Prayer-books. The firm make a speciality of the manufacture of account books, and keeps all varieties, strongly bound, in stock. Leather goods, including bags, purses, pocket-books, etc., are also largely represented, as also are fancy and useful articles suitable for presents.

A large wholesale trade is carried on in paper and stationery, throughout Worcestershire and the neighbouring counties; and a glance at the firm's Price List will show that they can sell as cheaply as any of the London or Birmingham houses. Another important department of the business is devoted to genuine patent medicines and proprietory articles, which are supplied at 'store prices.' In the foregoing account we have given the reader no idea of the endless variety of the stock held by Messrs. Lewis & Son, which must be seen to be properly appreciated. Orders by post or applications for samples, etc., receive special attention.

THE CITY AND COUNTY LAUNDRY
Proprietor: Mr. H. Griffiths
Arboretum Road, Worcester

No better locality could be suggested for the purposes of a high-class laundry than the site occupied by the above-named establishment, a part of the city lying in the direction of Barbourne, and singularly free from smoke or smuts so inimical in most suburban drying grounds. The business was established some four years ago by the present proprietor, Mr. H. Griffiths, who, with his wife, personally superintends every detail of the work.

The City and County Laundry was transferred last September to the present site in Arboretum Road, the building, formerly erected for a skating rink, being in every respect well adapted for the purpose. The portion of the structure occupied is the centre, and comprises a lofty and well-lighted building 50 feet in width, and 120 feet in length, giving ample space for the work of the various departments. The laundry is provided with every requisite in the form of appliances, and is heated by stoves of improved make for the indoor drying. All the work is performed by hand, no machinery being used in the various processes, and all chemicals and injurious materials are strictly tabooed in favour of the good, old-fashioned soap, soda, starch, and plenty of water and 'elbow grease.'

All kinds of general laundry work are undertaken, including ladies', gentlemen's, and household linens, blankets, quilts, curtains, and table napery, got up in faultless style, as may be inferred from the fact that the firm are employed by the residents at the Deanery, Malvern College, and similarly important institutions in the county. Customer's goods are collected and delivered in the well-appointed vans belonging to the laundry, which travel to all parts of the city and surrounding districts, where a large and influential connection has been established by the proprietors. As evidencing the excellence of the work carried out at the City and County Laundry, it should be mentioned that Mr. Griffiths was awarded a Prize Medal at the Fourth Annual Laundry Exhibition, held at the Royal Agricultural Hall, in 1896.

THE CITY AND COUNTY LAUNDRY

MR. J. S. COOK

Steam Printer, Account Book Maker, Bookbinder
'Reliance' Works, 47, Foregate Street, Worcester

This well-known business, which ranks among the chief of its kind in Worcestershire, was founded in 1880 by the present proprietor, Mr. J. S. Cook, under whose able management it has had a career of remarkable success, having come to the front rank of similar concerns in the short space of 16 years. Anyone who has inspected Mr. Cook's work, either in printing, Account Book Making, or bookbinding, will not be surprised that he should have gained the confidence of the public so rapidly. The testimonials he has received from clergymen, literary men, and others, afford abundant evidence of the opinion of the work produced by him.

The premises, which are centrally situated in Foregate Street, near the Railway Station, Victoria Institute, Post Office, etc., comprise a neat office on the ground floor, with spacious works in the rear. The latter are replete with the most modern printing, ruling, and bookbinding machines, and afford ample facilities for carrying on operations upon a very extensive scale. The premises are lighted by electricity and gas, the motive power employed being a modern 'Stockport,' gas engine. All classes of printing are undertaken, and orders are executed in an uniformly excellent style, displaying rare taste and expert workmanship in every detail. Account-book making and bookbinding both receive special attention, and in these branches Mr. Cook distinctly excels, alike on the score of quality and of price. Indeed, in all departments exceptionally moderate charges are made, although excellence of workmanship is never sacrificed to cheapness. The success of the house is undoubtedly largely due to the principal, Mr. Cook.

MR COOK'S PREMISES

MR. EDWARD SALLIS
Cheese, Bacon, and Butter Factor
47 High Street, Worcester

The oldest established house in the provision trade in Worcester is that conducted by Mr. Edward Sallis, which has throughout its long career enjoyed an unrivalled reputation, alike for the superior character of its products, and for the honourable principles upon which it is conducted. The business was founded more than a century ago, and during its career has had the honour of holding the Royal Appointment to Her late Majesty, Queen Adelaide.

The present proprietor, Mr. Sallis, has had the business for five years, and during this period he has more than sustained its reputation, and has extended its connections in all directions. The premises, which are centrally situated in High Street, comprise a handsome double-fronted shop, of most inviting appearance. Here may be seen a splendid stock of Wilts and Cumberland hams and bacon, Paysandu and pickled tongues, English and foreign cheese of the choicest descriptions, fresh butter, and other prime provisions. Of these, fresh supplies are being constantly received from dairy farms in all parts of the country. Mr. Sallis is agent for Hillier's sausages and Tebbutt's celebrated Melton pies, of which dainties, he has always a fine selection. Although excellence of quality is made the first consideration, Mr. Sallis's prices will be found exceptionally moderate. A number of smart assistants are employed, and all orders being executed with care and promptitude. A very extensive and influential business is in operation among the best classes of customers in Worcester, and for many miles round, there being deliveries daily throughout the district.

MR SALLIS' PREMISES

MESSRS. RUTTER & JONES
General Drapery, Dressmaking and Mourning Establishment
Compton House, 97, High Street, Worcester

Among the more recent aspirants to popular favour in the business firms of Worcester must be instanced Messrs. Rutter & Jones, General Drapers, Dressmakers, and Mourning Outfitters. The members of the firm have had a long experience in the business, Mr. Rutter having been for seventeen years manager of the largest drapery establishments in the town, and he thus acquired a wide experience now utilised to advantage in forwarding the interests of his own firm.

The establishment, known as 'Compton House,' is situated at 97, High Street, and has an attractive double frontage to that leading thoroughfare in which is presented a choice selection in all the smartest and most up-to-date novelties and styles for ladies' wear, in dress pieces, costumes, and general draperies of the first quality marked at exceedingly moderate prices. The interior is suitably furnished for the display of the large and varied stock of goods held in each department. On the upper floors are spacious and well-lighted work-rooms, wherein an efficient staff of experienced dress and mantle hands are employed in the completion of customers orders for costumes, mantles, and other outfitting in this line.

MESSRS RUTTER & JONES' PREMISES

Special care and attention are devoted to the execution of family mourning orders, in which the facilities at the firms' disposal, and Mr. Rutter's extensive experience in this department, enable them to compete, in point of economy and prompt despatch, with any house in the city.

JOSIAH STALLARD, & SONS, LTD.
Wine Merchants to the Queen
High Street, Worcester

This firm is an exceptionally old one and well known, it having been founded in the year 1808. The founder of the concern was Mr. William Stallard, who was succeeded by his son, the late Alderman Josiah Stallard, D. L., so that the control of the business has been in the hands of three generations of the same family. The firm have received Royal support, a distinction, we believe, which no other provincial firm of wine merchants in England possesses. The fine block of buildings they now occupy in High Street, was erected about 17 years ago. The structure is worthy of the eminent traditions of the house, while the vaults are among the most extensive owned by any firm in the kingdom. They cover an area of 11,000 square feet, and stretch from Copenhagen Street to Fish

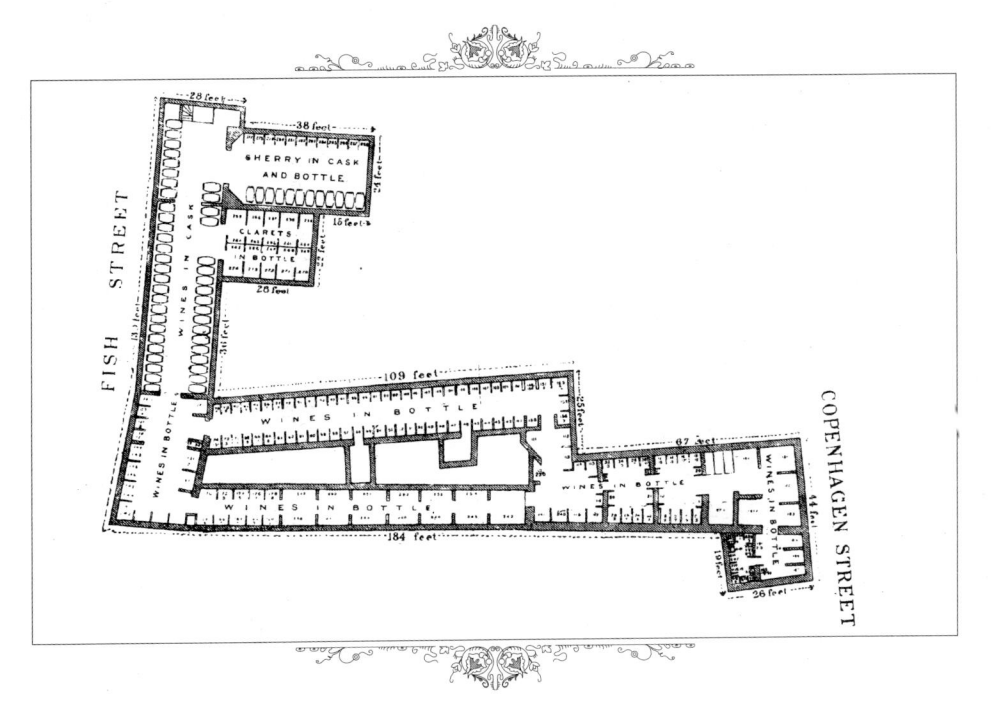

PLAN OF THE WINE CELLARS

Street, and from St. Helen's Church to St. Albans. On a recent visit of inspection we found these subterranean stores admirably planned and organised, the plan of storage being all that could be desired.

Of the bins the name is legion, and each is carefully numbered in correspondence with the bin books. Not an inch of space is wasted; indeed the economy exercised is one of the most striking features of the stores. The principal corridor, or long vault, is stocked with Port, Sherry, Hock, Claret, and other wines in cask and bottle. For the information of the connoisseur we may say that Messrs. Stallard have probably the largest of fine old Vintage Ports in the kingdom. With a view to the economising of space Messrs. Stallard have adopted the most improved methods of storage, and to this end have abandoned the older methods of immersing in sawdust. After inspecting the bottled wines department we turn our steps to the generous liquids in cask. In the Sherry department are stored hundreds of dozens of the choicest vintages that Xeres can supply, while in another store will be found innumerable cases of Champagne, still and sparkling Hocks, and other varieties of wine. On ascending once more to the ground floor the spirit room is likely to attract attention. Around this apartment are ranged casks of Brandy, Rum, Gin, Whisky, and Compounds; and attached to each cask is a gauge with figures printed thereon, which enables the fluid contents to be measured without the aid of the dipping rod. We pass to the Bonded Warehouses which are in Fish Street, adjoining the duty-paid cellars. These stores are under the supervision of Her Majesty's Excise officers. There is also a warehouse for bottling in bond for export trade.

But we must conclude our brief and utterly inadequate sketch, merely remarking that the house stands unrivalled in the Midlands. The present directors of the Company are Alderman John Stallard, J. P. (Worcester), Colonel and Alderman William Stallard (Worcester), T. B. Stallard, Esq., J. P. (Leominster). The Managing Director is J. Valentine Stallard, Esq., Chairman of the Worcester Board of Guardians.

The cellars may be viewed on application any day between the hours 8.10 a.m. and 5 p.m.

MESSRS. W. BENNETT & CO.
General Ironmongers, St Nicholas Street, Worcester

In the general ironmongery trade in Worcester, there is no house better known than that of W. Bennett, founded about sixteen years ago. The premises occupy a commanding site at the corner of St Nicholas Street and Queen Street, on the tram route between the Cross and Shrub Hill Station. The building is in pleasing architectural design, of red brick with stone dressings, and has a frontage of 80 feet to Queen Street. The interior is commodious and admirably arranged for the display of samples of the large and comprehensive stock. Space will prevent our alluding in detail to the various departments, but full particulars will be found in the admirably illustrated Price List, issued by the firm, which should be in the hands of every house-holder. The stock includes all kinds of furnishing ironmongery of the best manufacture; culinary utensils on the latest hygienic principles; horticultural implements of all kinds; sporting requisites; all descriptions of lamps, cutlery from leading London and Sheffield houses; electro-plated goods, etc., etc. Messrs. Bennett & Co. also deal extensively in builders' materials, including sanitary goods upon the most modern principles, and they have a particularly high reputation in this department. Their specialities in ranges consist of the 'Leamington,' 'Badger' and 'Eagle' lifting Fire Ranges, 'Mistress,' 'Hostess' and 'Treasure' Portable Ranges, which are among the best cooking ranges on the market. Competent workmen are sent any distance to fix the ranges in customers' houses. Builder's ironmongery of all kinds is kept in stock, including stoves of every description for coal, gas, or oil, also smokeless stoves, grates, chimney-pieces, locks, tile hearths, gas fittings, incandescent gas burners, galvanised roofing sheets, etc., etc. In all departments only the most moderate prices are charged, although excellence of quality is never sacrificed to cheapness.

MESSRS. BENNETT'S PREMISES

MR. W. STANLEY CARLESS, M.R.C.V.S.
Veterinary Surgeon
The Butts, Worcester

The increased attention devoted at the present day to the veterinary science is a most gratifying sign of the growing humanitarian instincts of the age. Indeed, to succeed now as a veterinary surgeon, more experience and skill are necessary than were a few years ago considered sufficient to equip a man to practise the healing art upon his fellows. This is as it should be, especially in a country like England, where every man delights to keep his horse and his dog, and looks upon these dumb friends as among the most precious of his belongings.

In Worcester the profession of veterinary surgeon is admirably represented, and we can select no more popular member of it for special mention than Mr. W. Stanley Carless, whose skill is beyond all dispute. Mr. Carless is a member of the Royal College of Veterinary Surgeons, and has attained a skill that few approach to. At his commodious premises, at the Butts, he has a capitally arranged 'hospital' for horses, dogs, and other animals, together with a well equipped surgery.

Mr. Carless has the reputation of being an experienced operator. Attached to the premises is a spacious shoeing forge, where a number of expert farriers and smiths are employed. Owners of valuable horses find it far safer to send them to an establishment of this class to be shod than to an ordinary shoeing forge. In all departments Mr. Carless has a large and influential connection.

MR CARLESS' 'HOSPITAL'

MISS A. M. PARMITER
School of Church and Art Embroidery
9 High Street, Worcester

Worcester, with its artistic and ecclesiastical associations, is eminently suited to be the seat of such an establishment as that described above. The Worcester School of Church and Art Embroidery is one of the institutions of the city, and has been extensively copied in other parts of the kingdom, but it has maintained its prestige, and its productions are in demand all over the country. Under the able management of Miss Parmiter the reputation of the school has been still further enhanced, and its connections extended in all directions. Every visitor to Worcester who takes delight in 'things of beauty,' should visit the showrooms of the school in High Street. Art needlework has, of late years, received the attention which it deserves, and every lady is expected to be deft with her needle. We were, however, agreeably surprised to find to what a height the art had been brought, when we visited Miss Parmiter's establishment. Many of the specimens shown to us displayed remarkable originality in conception, and exquisite taste in execution. We were particularly struck by the beautifully embroidered ecclesiastical ornaments, stoles, frontals, banners, etc. Beautiful figure work is produced, for which the school is deservedly famous, as well as work intended for domestic ornamentation. Space precludes our even referring to the chief items of the stock, but full particulars will be found in the admirable Catalogue and Price List, issued by Miss Parmiter, which should be in the hands of every clergyman, and every householder who wishes to make his home beautiful. Miss Parmiter gives lessons in ecclesiastical and secular embroidery, and wood carving, and has very great success with all her pupils.

MISS PARMITER'S ESTABLISHMENT

'GARDNER'S'
'Warwick House,' 26 High Street, Worcester

A very important addition to the millinery and fancy drapery establishments, in Worcester, was made a few months ago, when Mr. Gardner opened his business in High Street; and the patronage he has already secured bears abundant evidence to the able and enterprising methods he has adopted in its management. The premises, which have been recently reconstructed, are centrally situated in High Street, nearly opposite the Guildhall, and are designated 'Warwick House.' The shop has a handsome double frontage, with spacious plate-glass windows, always dressed in the most attractive style, with a splendid and varied assortment of the season's millinery in the most tasteful varieties and the latest French styles. Another noteworthy speciality of this establishment is the attention given to mourning millinery, besides one of the large windows devoted exclusively to this important branch, there is always a complete and well-arranged stock in hand; orders are executed on the shortest notice in a style displaying exquisite taste in every detail, and with the utmost punctuality.

There is a long tessellated arcade entrance, which leads to the commodious and well-appointed shop, which is brilliantly illuminated at night by electric incandescent lights. Above the shop are the work-rooms, where a number of thoroughly experienced assistants are engaged in the production of stylish millinery. The changes of modes are carefully followed, and ladies will find novelties here as soon as they appear. The general stock includes millinery trimmings in an extensive variety in all the most stylish and newest blends of colours; artificial flowers, feathers, a well-assorted stock of hosiery, reliable makes in gloves, and every description of fancy drapery. All the goods will be found of very superior character,

'WARWICK HOUSE'

and are offered at prices which will compare most favourably with those of other establishments. Mr. Gardner has already secured the support of a large and influential clientele, and there is every indication of a very rapid growth of the business, which is conducted on the lines of 'small profits, quick returns and no credit.'

MESSRS. HARDY & PADMORE, LTD.,
Engineers and General Ironfounders, Worcester

Although more widely known as the seat of the lighter forms of manufacture, the ancient 'Cathedral City' contains in its midst other industries of no less importance, from a utilitarian point of view, such as that established by Messrs. Hardy & Padmore, whose extensive manufactures of ranges, stoves, manholes, and general ironmongery and hardware of a heavier class give them a claim to rank with the principal representatives of this trade in the district. Originally founded in 1814, the firm has steadily developed the business as engineers and ironfounders, which now gives employment to upwards of two hundred hands in its various departments.

The works, situated in a part of the city known as the 'Blockhouse,' a central position on the borders of the Worcester and Birmingham Canal, are designed on the ground floor plan, and cover a very considerable area of ground, on which are erected ranges of extensive buildings, wherein are carried out the several branches of industry incidental to the work of production. The premises comprise large foundry, smith's forge, and fitting and machine shops, each replete with first-class modern plant, embodying all the latest possible improvements in machinery, tools

A HARDY & PADMORE ENGINE

and appliances for facilitating the output of the numerous specialities manufactured by the firm. These include kitchen ranges in what are known as the Yorkshire, Enclosed, Leamington, and other patterns of improved make, and a new design introduced by the firm, called the Improved Worcestershire Range. The house produce also some very elegant designs in register grates with over-mantles, tiled registers, stoves, manholes, garden rollers, furnaces, troughs, and every description of high-class ironmongery, sanitary, and architectural and engineering castings.

Full particulars of these goods are given in the well-illustrated catalogues and sectional price lists issued by Messrs. Hardy & Padmore, Ltd., to their customers, which will be found to contain more exact details of make, etc., than the limits of space at our disposal permit. An important speciality introduced by the firm a few years ago, is the 'Ideal' gas and oil engines constructed on Southall's patents. These engines are supplied, excepting as regards one small size, fitted up to work on the 'Otto' cycle, and are practically noiseless in action. The patented governor is very efficient and ensures the speed of the engines being most regular; the valve gear also allows of their running at very high speeds, rendering them specially suitable for driving dynamos. No skilled attention is required to use them, and the prices are extremely reasonable, their construction throughout being thoroughly substantial, and the workmanship in them is as good as it can be. These engines are recommended for driving small, light-running machines, such as ventilating propellers, coffee roasters, tea-mixers, shows, fans, models, advertisements, punkalis, hair brushes, grindstones, jeweller's lathes, meat choppers, boot brushes, drills, printing presses, chaff cutters, lathes, dynamos, and all light purposes requiring mechanical motive force. Numerous testimonials have been received by the makers from power users, expressive of the highest satisfaction with the 'Ideal' gas engine, as being regular in running, simple, efficient, and silent. Engines of this make have been supplied to buyers in Australia, Italy, France, Portugal, and Holland, and also in large numbers in all parts of the United Kingdom.

MR. JOHN ALFRED STEWARD
Dispensing Chemist, 27 High Street, Worcester

The increased attention devoted to hygienic matters at the present day has added considerably to the importance of the pharmaceutical profession, to succeed in which now, as much skill and knowledge are necessary as were once sufficient for the equipment of a fully qualified medical practitioner. Indeed, the family chemist is the legitimate successor of the old-time apothecary, and has been well named 'the physician of the poor.' One of the most notable chemist's establishments in Worcester is that conducted by Mr. John Alfred Steward, which dates back to 1776, when it was actually an apothecary's shop, and what is most interesting is that for many years it was carried on by a certain Mr. Featherstonhaugh, mentioned so often by Mrs. Henry Wood in her books. Mr. Steward acquired the business in 1876, and although he has thoroughly brought it up to date, the house still retains the reputation and dignity which belongs, by right, to a concern of this antiquity. The premises, which are centrally situated in High Street, comprise a handsome double-fronted shop, of somewhat old-fashioned appearance, but whose elegantly appointed interior is admirably adapted to modern requirements. A large and well-selected stock is held embracing the purest drugs and chemicals; genuine patent medicines and proprietary articles; medical and surgical appliances upon the most improved principles, and toilet and nursery requisites of the best manufacture. Full particulars of these will be found in the comprehensive and admirably printed Price List issued by Mr. Steward, from which it will be gathered that his charges compare very favourably with those of the various co-operative stores. Special attention is devoted to dispensing, for which only drugs and chemicals of absolute purity, according to the British Pharmacopoeia, are used. In this department the house

MR JOHN STEWARD

enjoys the confidence of the leading physicians in Worcester and district. Mr. J. A. Steward is one of the best known and most respected residents in the city, and is a most useful, though quiet, member of the Council, representing the ward of All Saints.

MR JOHN STEWARD'S HIGH STREET SHOP

MR. A. O. MAINWARING

Family Grocer and Italian Warehouseman,

The Cathedral Tea and Coffee Warehouse,

College Street, Worcester

All the advantages of the modern cash system of trading are realised in purchasing supplies of grocery and provisions from the well-known establishment, familiar to the Worcester public as 'The Cathedral Tea and Coffee Warehouse,' of which the enterprising proprietor, Mr. A. O. Mainwaring, has adopted the policy of purveying only the best possible quality of goods at the lowest prices for ready money, in preference to the old-fashioned method of giving long credits, so frequently so disastrous to both seller and buyer, as its title suggests; the establishment is situated beneath the shadow of the venerable fane of which Worcester is so justly proud, occupying a commanding corner position at the junction of College Street and Lich Street.

The premises are commodious and well appointed and arranged, the building of four-storey elevation in red brick having an excellent window frontage to both thoroughfares mentioned, with entrance at the corner surmounted by a sign board inscribed with the name of the establishment:- 'The Cathedral Tea and Coffee Warehouse and General Grocery Stores.' The stocks in each of these departments are selected with the greatest care from the leading markets, and represent in the principal specialities teas of the highest order of excellence, the proprietor devoting a large amount of time and attention to this important branch of the business in obtaining the best and choicest qualities of China, Indian, and Ceylon teas, and these are blended with discriminating judgement, so as to combine strength with delicacy of flavour. The teas range in price from 1 shilling per lb. to a remarkably fine quality 'Ye Tea of ye Olden Time' at 3s.10d. (such as our forefathers did 'drinke and enjoie'). The Coffees are of similar superiority, being roasted twice a week, and fresh ground every morning ensuring all the essentials of a delicious cup of this refreshing beverage. In general groceries the stocks are complete with all articles embraced in the comprehensive category of Italian Warehouse goods. Fuller details of these will be found duly set forth in the extensive Cash Price List issued by the proprietor, which contains much useful information of interest to the housekeeper, and should certainly find a place in all well-regulated residences where economy is considered of importance. Families are waited upon for orders in a service of well organised rounds, embracing all parts of the city and surrounding districts where Mr. Mainwaring has established a very extensive and influential connection in supplying private residents and wholesale buyers.

MR. C. HANCOCK
Steam Joinery Works and Moulding Mills
Charles Street, Worcester

In the wood-making industry, in Worcester, there is no name better known than that of Mr. C. Hancock, who, for nearly a quarter of a century, has been engaged in this important trade, in which he has made for himself and unrivalled reputation, alike for the excellence of his productions and for the strict integrity which characterises all his transactions. The premises are situated in Charles Street, in the midst of that industrial quarter of the city, which so few visitors see, and, in consequence, carry away an erroneous notion as to the industrial resources of Worcester.

The works are quite close to the Birmingham and Worcester Canal, which affords admirable facilities for transport purposes. We have visited few joinery works so completely equipped as those of Mr. Hancock. We noticed horizontal, circular, and band saws, lathes, moulding, morticing, planing and other machines, in the latest designs, and of the best manufacture, affording ample facilities for carrying on in any department of the wood-working industry. The machinery is all driven by steam power, a fine engine being employed. A large number of experienced hands are engaged in the works, which present at all times a scene of great activity. Mr. Hancock manufactures all classes of joinery work for builders, the leading firms of whom in Worcester and for many miles round, draw their supplies from him. A speciality is made of the Secret Joint Dado Boarding, of which he is the sole manufacturer in Worcester. Another important feature of the business is antique oak carved panelling for Dados. Doors are also a speciality, and in this department, in reference alike to price and excellence of workmanship, Mr. Hancock can defy competition. He is also noted for sashes and frames, cucumber frames, and melon pits, with which he supplies market gardeners and private growers throughout the Midlands. Greenhouses are erected to order, upon the most modern principles. Great care is devoted to the seasoning of all the wood used, which is dried by natural and not artificial processes. Estimates, in any department, are submitted upon application, and will be found exceptionally moderate. To the foregoing remarks we may add that Mr. Hancock is the sole manufacturer of an improved Fire-Lighter, the combustible properties of which are superior to anything of the kind we have noticed in the market. Mr. Hancock has evidently solved the problem- 'How to avoid waste,' and thereby has effected an economy that the public will not be slow to appreciate. These Fire-Lighters are made from joinery chippings, such as oak, pitch-pine, and red deal; they save time and labour, and risks are avoided in houses by their use, no smells being developed, nor sparks shot about to the danger of property and person. Mr. Hancock on the 22nd February 1897, purchased the premises, which he has uninterruptedly occupied since August 1872, and we understand it is his intention to effect many important alterations, and to introduce additional machinery and appliances of the most improved description. We heartily wish the proprietor the degree of success to which his undoubted energy and enterprise so justly entitle him.

MR HANCOCK'S WORKS

MR. CHAS. F. BROWN
LATE
HENRY BROWN,
Monumental Sculptor, Granite, Stone and Marble Works
St. Nicholas Street, Worcester

'Yet e'en these bones from insult to protect.'

The raising of some kind of memorial to the dead seems an act which is inherent in the human race. Indeed, the only remains we have of races which once inhabited this world, take the form of tumuli, pyramids, or monuments, raised in respect to their departed. The monumental mason may, therefore, claim to belong to the oldest craft in the world, and in these matter-of-fact, and materialistic days, he still holds his own, and his services are ever in demand. In connection with this profession in Worcester, there is no name better known than that which heads this brief sketch. The family of Mr. C. F. Brown, has been engaged in the craft for three generations, so that he inherits his remarkable skill as a monumental mason. If asked for evidence of the ability of his house, he might point to the churches, cemeteries, and churchyards in all parts of the midlands, and say, in the words of the epitaph of the great architect, *'circumspice.'* Monuments signed by the name of Brown may be seen in Worcester Cathedral as well as in churches of lesser note. All the work will be found of the most artistic description, and displays great beauty of finish. Many of the designs are quite original, and stamp their producers as men of no ordinary skill and taste. Mr. Brown's works are conveniently situated in St. Nicholas Street, and are admirably adapted to the requirements of the trade. Designs and estimates are submitted upon application, and the charges will be found of the most moderate description. A number of skilled hands assist Mr. Brown, and all orders are executed on the shortest notice.

MR. CHARLES BURDEN
Botanic Dispensary
35, Broad Street, Worcester

The efficacy of herbs and roots as healing agents has been acknowledged from the earliest agents; and there are no safer nor less harmless remedies known than those supplied by the medical botanist. It is not within our province here to argue in favour of herbs versus chemicals as medicines, although we could advance many weighty, and in our opinion, unanswerable facts in favour of the former. In this place we simply draw attention to an admirably conducted Botanic Dispensary, which has flourished in Worcester for the past ten years, under the able management of Mr. Charles Burden, who is a member of the National Association of Medical Herbalists of Great Britain.

Mr. Burden's premises are conveniently situated in Broad Street, near the Severn Bridge. They comprise a neat shop, with well arranged laboratory attached. All kinds of herbs used for medicinal purposes are kept in stock, and herbal prescriptions are dispensed with great care, only the best ingredients being used. Mr. Burden is the proprietor of several valuable specifics, which decidedly enjoy a very wide-spread repute. Among these, we may mention his Botanic Embrocation and Herbal syrup for indigestion - the latter, a sovereign remedy against that troublesome complaint.

Notice should not be omitted of Burden's Botanic Liver Pills, which speedily cure all stomachic and liver complaints. These pills have stood the test of fifty years' sale, with ever-increasing popularity. They are made from herbs which are known to have direct curative action upon the stomach and liver. Mr. Burden has a very successful practice among all classes in Worcester, and for several miles round the city.

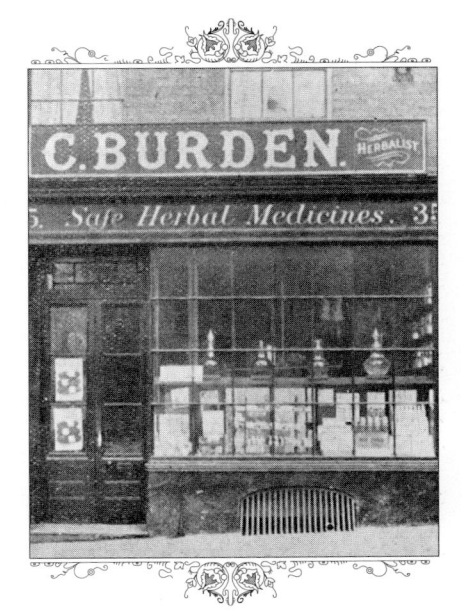

MR BURDEN'S PREMISES

MR. W. BURTON
Practical Hunting Saddler
The Butts, Worcester

Worcestershire enjoys a high reputation among hunting men, and among the leading industries of the town we should naturally expect to find that of saddlery and harness-making. This business is certainly well represented, the chief concern of the kind, being that so ably conducted by Mr. W. Burton, which can point to a record of more than twenty years of unqualified success. Mr. Burton has himself had invaluable experience in the trade, having formerly been with the famous house of Wilkinson & Co., London. The premises, which are conveniently situated at the Butts, comprise a double-fronted shop, well arranged as a show-room, with spacious and well equipped works attached. A large number of skilled operatives are employed; and all orders are executed on the shortest notice, in a style displaying expert and finished workmanship in every detail.

Mr. Burton pays great attention to the manufacture of hunting, racing, and military saddles, and supplies the leading masters of hounds, nobility and gentry, and the local cavalry and volunteer throughout the Midland Counties. He is also prepared to measure and carefully fit horses with the most improved harness and clothing. Only the very best materials are used, and for excellence of appearance and durability the productions of this house are not to be surpassed. The business is in every way admirably managed, and reflects the highest credit upon its enterprising proprietor.

MR BURTON'S PREMISES

MR. W. NAPPER
Fancy Drapery and Trimming Warehouse,
87, High Street, Worcester

The constantly varying decrees of Dame Fashion in those articles of feminine embellishment, comprised in the description of fancy drapery and trimmings, are illustrated in perfectly up-to-date form at the well-known establishment of Mr. W. Napper, whose display of this class of goods is at all times fully replete with the latest novelties in each department as soon as they are introduced by the principal London and Paris houses. Having the advantage of many years experience in the trade, Mr Napper possesses discriminating judgment in the selection of suitable goods, and as he has been established in the business for over twenty years, he may certainly claim a recognised standing as one of the most popular caterers in this connection in the 'Faithful City.' The establishment occupies a central position at 87, High Street, near the Guild Hall, and has a handsome and attractive double front, the windows at all times presenting a most alluring display of articles incidental to the trade, the effect in the evening being heightened by an installation of the electric light in groups and pendant incandescent globes. Entering through an arcade doorway, with tessellated pavement, the visitor is ushered into the spacious interior, well-appointed and furnished, fitted with the usual counters and other fixtures of modern design. The stocks are perfectly comprehensive in character, and may be said to embrace every article included in the category of fancy drapery and trimmings to meet every requirement of decoration for a lady`s indoor and outdoor toilette, together with laces, gloves, lingerie, etc., the whole forming a very charming display of high-class goods unexcelled in quality and variety of choice by that of any other

MR NAPPER'S PREMISES

house in the City. The contents of the several departments are constantly recruited with new season specialities and styles, Mr. Napper personally visiting the chief centres of fashion in his periodical buying journeys. The establishment has long enjoyed the patronage of a wide circle of influential customers among the best class of Worcester residents, and to a large extent, supplies the requirements of wholesale buyers, such as dressmakers, mantle makers and costumiers in the district.

BARTHOLOMEW`S BATHS AND HYDROPATHIC ESTABLISHMENT
Mr. W. Park, Proprietor, Sansome Walk, Worcester

Of late years increased attention has been devoted by the medical faculty to hydropathy in all its branches, and it has been found that water-cure surpasses in efficacy, in a very large number of diseases, all that could possibly be accomplished by drugs, without the evil effects which attend indulgence in the latter. Indeed, medical science is every year coming more into accord with Macbeth`s famous dictum 'Throw physic to the dogs.' In Worcester the hydropathic treatment of diseases has long received careful attention, and the city boasts one of the most important establishments devoted to it, to be met with in the Kingdom. We refer to Bartholomew`s Baths and Hydropathic Establishment, which was founded twenty years ago. It has been for eight years in the possession of Mr W. Park, who has devoted great attention to the study of his profession and is assisted by his wife, who, like himself, holds the highest testimonials as to ability and efficacy in the administration of every description of hydropathic and Turkish bath treatment.

Under Mr. Park`s auspices the whole establishment has been altered and improved, and it is now one of the most complete concerns of the kind in the Kingdom. The baths and hydropathic are situated in one of the best parts of Worcester, and consist of twenty rooms used by patients as boarders, or let in suites or apartments to persons taking the baths, or to visitors and tourists.

The baths include Turkish, hot and cold water, swimming, Droitwich brine, sulphur, mercurial, electric, pine-oil fomentations, oxygen inhalations, and other hydropathic and special treatments. Patients come from all parts of the United Kingdom, and have proved that, in point of cure, more has been done here in one week than in any other curative establishment in three weeks. Mrs. Park and Mr. Park are both certified medical rubbers, and are prepared to do massage, and rubbing, on the premises or by appointment. An experienced chiropodist is always in attendance. Space precludes our dwelling at greater length on this excellent establishment, but full particulars may be obtained from Mr. Park`s pamphlet, describing the action of Turkish baths, and giving testimonials, and terms of board, lodging, and treatment.

MR. PARK'S BATHING ESTABLISHMENT

THE MIDLAND DRAPERY CO.
General Drapers, 42, High Street, Worcester

One of the most attractive features that meets the eye of the pedestrian who walks along Worcester's principal thoroughfare is the large drapery warehouse which we name at the head of this sketch. The house is known far and wide, partly by reason of its business motto, and trade mark, both of which indicate very manifestly the thorough go-ahead and enterprising spirit that actuates the management. The model of a huge magnet, suspended over the entrance, bears along with it the suggestive words 'The Magnet that draws the People,' and this magnet, we may remark here, expresses sound quality allied with true cheapness, the latter being a matter that by no means necessarily implies lowness of price. Indeed nothing could be more misleading than to suppose that cheapness consisted in this latter particular; on the contrary low-priced goods are not uncommonly the dearest in the market. The Midland Drapery Company, by combining the highest excellence of value with the lowest prices commensurate with sound business stability, have indeed provided a magnet that draws the public.

The establishment is spacious and has a long rearward extension, together with two fine galleries at the lower end, which enhance the storage capacity of the business. Seldom have we seen a better-lighted drapery emporium, and the staff of assistants, headed by a genial and able manager, make it a pleasure to deal at the house. Courtesy is a keynote here, and we speak as we found it, and not with any desire to indulge in fulsome words of commendation. The basement, too, contains heavy stocks, and during the Christmas Season we understand the Midland Drapery Company devote this floor to the purposes of a showroom for toys, dolls, and fancy articles much in evidence during that festive season.

The secret of the Company's undoubted success is not far to seek. The most advanced business methods are brought to bear in the management, and the buying is effected in such enormous parcels as to really command the market, and selling, as the Company does, for cash, it stands to reason that the rapid turnover enables the administration to give every advantage to the customer. Every department of drapery is here fully represented, and all the goods we noticed on the occasion of our visit abundantly testify to the capability of those engaged in the difficult task of buying. We gladly hail the Midland Drapery Company as a decided acquisition to the trade and industry of the 'Faithful City.'

THE MIDLAND DRAPERY COMPANY

MESSRS. HEATH & SON
Sanitary Plumbers, Gasfitters, Painters,
House Decorators
2, St. Swithin Street, Worcester

The close attention now directed to every branch of sanitary science has erected the plumber's industry to a position almost unique in importance as affecting the health of the community in all large centres of population, where neglect of these essential precautions was formerly a prolific cause of preventible disease.

The advance made in the direction of improvement in matters connected with house drainage, and more efficient methods of construction and ventilation has been consistently followed by the well-known firm of Messrs. Heath & Son, sanitary plumbers, gasfitters, house decorators, etc., who for nearly half-a-century past, have successfully specialised these branches in which they are justly recognised as practical experts.

Occupying a conveniently central site in St Swithin Street, near the Cross, the firm's premises consist of a neat and compact shop with single-window frontage in which is displayed an assortment of new and artistic designs in wall papers and

MESSRS. HEATH & SON'S PREMISES

decorative materials for dining room, drawing-room, bedroom, hall and staircase in a great variety of tones and tints to harmonise with the prevailing styles of interior embellishment. A good selection is also shown of pumps, bath and lavatory fittings, wash-down and other closets, and all the most improved appliances and requisites for sanitary drainage. The industrial departments are carried out in well equipped workshops, and a staff of skilful and competent hands are employed in the various branches in progress.

The principal features of the out-door work undertaken are the inspection of drainage systems and the preparation of reports with a view to effecting sanitary improvements, a branch of the business conscientiously and satisfactorily performed under the immediate personal supervision of the principals in order to ensure perfect efficiency in the arrangements in conformity with the regulations of the local authorities. Messrs. Heath & Son, also submit schemes of interior and exterior decoration for public and private buildings, for which estimates are prepared for painting, paperhanging, colouring, white-washing, shop front decorations, glass and other sign writing, at a very reasonable scale of charges.

MESSRS. GEORGE & WELCH
Family and Dispensing Chemists, Worcester

An interesting survival of this fine old city is furnished in the quaint establishment of Messrs. George & Welch, who probably enjoy one of the largest practices as pharmaceutical chemists in this part of the Midlands. Originally founded over a century ago, the business was acquired by the present proprietors, some thirty years since - the members of the firm, as now constituted, being Mr. H. George, and Mr. W. H. Maxey, formerly with Messrs. Savory and Moore, chemists to the Queen. The establishment is advantageously situated in one of the principal business thoroughfares of the city. A feature of interest in the windows is a row of the old-fashioned jars in which the apothecary of by-gone days used to store the medicaments then in vogue. The interior arrangements are, throughout, in keeping with the ancient appearance of the place. The antiquity of the surroundings, however, only serve to accentuate the up-to-date character of the stock, which embraces all the leading specialities now supplied at a high-class pharmaceutical establishment, including all the best and purest qualities of drugs and chemicals used in the dispensing department, wherein prescriptions are compounded by experienced assistants. Among the list of specialties prepared by the firm, and widely known for their uniformly high standard of excellence and successful circulation, are included an extensive range of dietary articles of extra strength and purity, patent medicines, fancy soaps, and surgical and medical requirements, all of which are stocked in infinite variety.

Of these, attention may be directed to the following:- Liver Pills; Liver Tonic, which may be taken with advantage with the pills; Red Currant Linctus, for coughs, colds, etc.: Liquid Almond Cream and Soap, specifics for removing skin imperfections; Carbolic Cream, healer and purifier for the cure of Eczema, and other skin diseases, burns, etc.; Petroleum Pomade, for preserving and darkening the hair; Anti-septic Eau de Cologne (a hygienic mouthwash); Carboline Sanitary Tooth Paste; Aromatic Carbolic Tooth Powder; Dentrifices of rose, violet and Quinine; Locock's Stimulant; Wilson's Restorative and hair lotions. Some highly excellent culinary preparations are also prepared by the firm, including Indian Meat Seasoning, Currie Powder, Salad Oil and Cream, Malt, Tarragon and Chillic Vinegars, mustard, spices, sauces, peppers, ketchups, and other condiments of the finest quality obtainable.

Numerous testimonials have been received by the firm from purchasers of these specialities, expressing unqualified satisfaction with their efficacy and usefulness for the several purposes to which they are applied.

MESSRS. GEORGE & WELCH'S PREMISES

THE WORCESTER GENERAL POSTING ESTABLISHMENT
Proprietors: Messrs, Shipway & Hughes
London Road, Hop Market Hotel Stables, and Dutton Street, Rainbow Hill

Residents and visitors alike in the 'Faithful City' desirous of obtaining well-appointed vehicles, for either pleasure or business purposes, will find their requirements fully satisfied on application to Messrs. Shipway & Hughes, proprietors of 'the original and only' Worcester General Posting Establishments, which are among the best equipped and largest concerns of the kind in the Midlands. The business is of over forty years standing in the city, and has been in the hands of the present proprietors for the past fifteen years, during which time, under their more energetic and enterprising management, the trade has been very considerably extended by opening up new branches in various parts of the district.

The head-quarters of the firm are in London Road, a short distance from town in the direction of Red Hill, where a handsome block of red brick buildings has been erected replete with every modern convenience for a large business of this character. The premises consists of a spacious paved yard, flanked on either side by well-constructed stables, loose boxes, lock-up coaches, harness room, and the necessary stores for corn, forage, etc. The rolling stock includes elegant landaus and broughams for wedding parties, large brakes and four-in-hand coaches for picnic parties, waggonettes, hansom cabs, and open and closed vehicles of all kinds, which are turned out in first-class style at moderate charges.

A splendid stud of hunters hacks and harness horses are placed at the disposal of the firm's customers, and may be hired by the day, week, month, or year, the animals being invariably in the pink of condition, and sent out well-groomed and fully equipped with the best quality of saddlery and harness for whatever purpose required. Competent and thoroughly trustworthy drivers only are placed in charge of the vehicles lent on hire, and these are supplied in neat liveries when required. Special attention is given to the vehicles employed for funerals, the firm being sole proprietors of the new patent hearse, and supplying also shillibears and broughams of modern construction, horsed with some fine specimens of the Belgium breed in full black entire animals.

The branch establishments are at the Hop Market Hotel, in the centre of the city, Dutton Street and Rainbow Hill, all of which are equally well provided with horses and vehicles obtainable at short notice; and special orders can be promptly forwarded to headquarters by means of the telephone which has been established by private wire between the various offices. The entire details of the management are subject to the personal supervision of the proprietors, both of whom possess a thoroughly practical knowledge of the requirements of the trade, enabling them to give invariable satisfaction to their numerous and influential clients among the nobility, clergy, and resident gentry in the neighbourhood.

The firm are also dealers and trainers of horses, and also dealers in all kinds of carriages. Trial allowed, and every guarantee given.

THE WORCESTER GENERAL POSTING ESTABLISHMENT

CARMICHAEL & SONS
Coach Builder, The Butts, Worcester

It is nearly approaching upon fifty years since the business, now carried on by Messrs. Carmichael & Son, of the Butts, Worcester, was founded. The business passed into the hands of its present principal, some twenty-three years ago, and it is since that period that the progressive character of the concern's operations have been chiefly observable. The building occupied by Messrs. Carmichael & Son is most substantially constructed of red brick, and comprises two storeys, the showroom being on the ground floor. At rear and on the upper part of the premises are located the workshops, the bodymakers, upholsterers and painting shops are on the upper floors for further treatment in their gradual course of construction and finish. There are also sheds for the storage of timber, iron, and other heavy material necessary to the business. A glance through the showroom will afford convincing proof that the firm turn out work of the highest style and finish, both as regards construction and workmanship. Messrs. Carmichael & Son are manufacturers of fine brakes for pleasure parties, landaus, phaetons, dogcarts, broughams, victorias and other fashionable vehicles, together with carts and vans of every description. We were much impressed on the occasion of our visit with a particularly taking vehicle suited to the special requirements of medical men, light running, easy, yet durable, with safe steps and nice roomy seats, in fact the very *beau ideal* of a comfortable vehicle. Fitted with noiseless axles and a brake for hilly countries, we are sure that such a carriage is the very thing to meet the requirements of residents in and medical practitioners of the district of which the 'Faithful City' form the natural centre. The firm have many more such interesting specimens of their handiwork and to exhibit these to visitors is at all times a pleasure to the esteemed principal.

A CARMICHAEL COACH

MESSRS. MUNT & COMPANY, LTD
Cabinetmakers, Upholsterers, Carpet Warehousemen
50, High Street, Worcester

At the present day artistic furniture and furnishings are within the reach of all classes of the community, with the result that English homes are decidedly lighter, prettier, and more tasteful than they have ever been before. Indeed, one can make one's house artistic for about half the price our father's paid to make it hideous with lumbering horse-hair furniture and gaudy lustre chandeliers! If one would see how near perfection the furnishing trade has now been brought, he would do well to pay a visit to the show rooms of Messrs. Munt & Co., Ltd., in High Street, Worcester.

This enterprising firm cater for all classes of the community, and are prepared to furnish throughout any residence, from a cottage to a mansion. Their premises occupy a fine site at the corner of High Street and Church Street, and have splendid frontages to both those important thoroughfares. The windows are most tastefully arranged, and when, after dark, the premises are illuminated with incandescent electric lamps, the effect is exceptionally brilliant. The interior extends back about 100 feet. There is a front show room abutting upon the above-mentioned thoroughfares, while behind this is another 'cabinet room' lighted from the roof, with galleries above for the display of the stock. It is seldom, indeed, that one meets so fine an assortment of furniture under one roof. Dining room, drawing room, and bedroom suites, in a variety of woods, but all of the most artistic designs and finished workmanship, are particularly well represented, as also are handsome cabinets and sideboards, tables, bookcases and occasional furniture of all descriptions.

The firm have also a splendid selection of carpets and curtains, in all the newest art patterns and shades, and from the most famous looms, affording customers a practically unlimited choice. Special attention is devoted to the taking up, beating, altering and re-laying of carpets. Messrs. Munt & Company have large workshops in New Street, where about forty experienced cabinet makers and upholsterers are employed. Orders for the repairing, re-polishing, and re-covering of furniture receive careful attention, and are executed on the shortest notice in a style displaying expert and finished workmanship in every detail. The house is also noted for artistic inside and outside blinds. We must also mention that the firm have a manufactory in New Street, where they manufacture bedding furniture of all kinds. In all departments an extensive business is carried on under the able and energetic management of Mr. C. H. Brown, to whom the success of the establishment is, in no small measure, due.

MESSRS. MUNT'S HIGH STREET PREMISES

MR. S. HILL

Umbrella Manufacturer, 22 & 23, New Street, Worcester

The uncertain climatic conditions peculiar to all parts of the British Isles render the possession of a reliable umbrella an indispensable requirement of personal equipment, and make provision for a 'rainy day' a duty which no self-respecting citizen would disregard. This may be done at the establishment of Mr. S. Hill, who, as an umbrella manufacturer, has a widespread repute for the consistent excellence of his goods.

Originally founded as far back as 1841, the business has had a long and prosperous career, which, under the direction of its present proprietor, has been continuously maintained with ever increasing success. The site occupied by Mr. Hill's establishment possesses no small measure of historical interest, being close to what is reported to be the houses from which King Charles escaped after the battle of Worcester in 1651. The more modern building adjoining, occupied by Mr. Hill, has a spacious window frontage, and well-appointed interior, the whole of the arrangements being perfectly up-to-date with the requirements of the business.

The stock includes umbrellas in silk and other materials, mounted on Fox's and the proprietor's own special paragon frames, all of which are manufactured on the premises by first-class workmen only, whose services are also available for re-covering, repairs, etc. A wide range of sunshades and *En-tout-cas* is also shown, together with a large assortment of walking sticks, india-rubber goods, footballs, bags, portmanteaus, dress baskets, and other details of a traveller's equipment for journeys at home or abroad.

A speciality of Mr. Hill's manufacture is an improved gig umbrella, strongly made to resist both rain and wind, and constructed of the best materials and workmanship; may be commended to those who have occasion to drive long distances in uncertain weather. All kinds of umbrellas are made to order, with sticks selected by the customer if desired, and in any description of silk or other covering. The establishment is the principal one in this trade in the city, and has long been the seat of an extensive and highly influential business.

Portrait of a Victorian City 127

MR. HILL'S PREMISES

THE END.

Established 1705 in Lincolnshire.

THE
BLACK PEAR BRAND.
Scotch Whiskies.

The following Whiskies having Matured in our own Bonded Stores, Boston, Lincolnshire, are of guaranteed Age and Purity.

1 Dozen (2 Gals.)

A FINE LIQUER WHISKY	48/-	Carriage Paid.
AVERAGE AGE 7 YEARS	42/-	,,
A GOOD BLEND	36/-	,,

E. RIDLINGTON,
Wine and Spirit Merchant,
WORCESTER.

ESTABLISHED OVER A QUARTER OF A CENTURY.

C. A. COOK,

Carver, Gilder, Picture Frame Maker, and Picture Restorer,

PHOTOGRAPHIC FRAME MANUFACTURER OF EVERY DESCRIPTION,

22, MEALCHEAPEN STREET,
- - WORCESTER. - -

Works—BACK OF 19 AND 22 MEALCHEAPEN STREET.